Pet Owner's Guide to
THE
DALMATIAN

Geraldine Gregory

HOWELL
BOOK HOUSE

NEW YORK

HOWELL BOOK HOUSE
A Prentice/Macmillan Company
15 Columbus Circle
New York, NY 10023

Library of Congress Cataloging-in-Publication data

Gregory, Geraldine.
  Pet owner's guide to the Dalmatian / by Geraldine Gregory.
  1st American ed.
      p.   cm.
  ISBN 0-87605-991-4
  1. Yorkshire terriers.   I. Title
  SF429.D3G74   1994   94-8530   CIP
  636.7'2   dc20

Manufactured in Hong Kong
10 9 8 7 6 5 4 3 2 1

Contents

The spectacular markings and lively personality of the Dalmatian make this breed a firm favourite with all dog lovers.

About the author

Geraldine Gregory has bred, exhibited and judged Dalmatians for nearly thirty years, and has enjoyed great success with her Spotarton prefix. She has made up a number of Champions, both black-spotted and liver-spotted, and has always ensured that her home-bred stock has excelled in the typical, fun-loving, outgoing temperament of the Dalmatian, which makes the breed so special.

Geraldine's dogs are always beautifully cared for, and she made breed history when one of her Champions qualified for the national Veteran Stakes five years in succession. On the last occasion, this male was also represented by his Champion son and daughter. Geraldine is an international Championship show judge, and she served on the committee for the North of England Dalmatian Club.

Acknowledgements

Photo credits: Russell Fine Art (page 4), A. Bale-Stock (pages 8, 56, 80).

Cover photograph: Double Dee from Dallyvista (pet name Jodie). Bred by Janet Shuttleworth, owned by Malcolm and Brenda Smith.

Photography: Carol Ann Johnson

Chapter One

THE DALMATIAN BREED

ORIGINS
Nobody really knows how the Dalmatian originated, but the 'spotted dog' has been around for a very long time – they were even depicted in the Egyptian tombs over 2,000 years ago. The 'spotted dog' has had a variety of names. In Buffon's work *Histoire Naturelle* (published c1750), it was referred to as the 'Braque de Bengale', which was a type of hunting hound. In records of the Viking invasion of Scotland, there is mention of a small Danish Dog, suggesting that it was a smaller version of the harlequin-coloured Great Dane.

But it is normally assumed that the breed originated from Dalmatia, on the eastern Adriatic coast, possibly taken there by travellers. The first reference to the breed by its now well-known name of Dalmatian is in Thomas Pennant's *Synopsis of Quadrupeds*, published in 1771.

HUNTING DOGS
Over the years the Dalmatian has been used in a variety of ways. The early spotted dogs were thought of as hounds, and were used for hunting. In fact, there have been occasions in recent years when Dalmatians have run with a pack of hounds, and have been fully accepted by both pack and the huntsmen, thus apparently reverting to their hound ancestry. Travelling gypsies were attracted by the breed's unusual appearance, and incorporated spotted dogs in their circus acts.

CARRIAGE DOGS
It was in the role of a coach or carriage dog that the Dalmatian became best-known. Dalmatians used to run with the carriages of the gentry, guarding the horses, the carriage and the occupants. If the journey extended overnight, the Dalmatians would spend the night in the stables keeping watch over the horses.

The dogs were useful as guards, but they were also valued for their distinctive appearance. It soon became a mark of high fashion among the gentry to have spotted dogs running behind the family carriage. A wood engraving by Thomas Bewick (c1790) depicts the Dalmatian as a Carriage Dog, and several other works from around 1800 show the breed in this role.

As horse-drawn carriages declined, so, of course, did the work of the Dalmatian. In America they were adopted in many places as mascots for the fire service, again running with the horse-drawn vehicles, and latterly sitting alongside the firemen when the internal combustion engine took over. The carriage dog of old became known the 'Fire Dog'.

Today, the Dalmatian is essentially a family companion, willing to fit into most ways of life, but always happiest when with the humans they own. They have been lovingly referred to, as 'plum pudding dogs', but to most youngsters (and some not so young) they will always be 'spotty dog'.

PUBLIC PROFILE

The Dalmatian's unusual and aristocratic appearance has resulted in the breed being in great demand for use in advertising campaigns and in films. The list of products the Dalmatian has lent its name to is vast, ranging from bricks and banking to food, clothes and jewellery. In photographic work, the Dalmatian fits in well, whether on his own or with a model. On television he comes over as a friendly addition to any message, making the product more memorable.

The film industry has also made use of the Dalmatian, especially in 'period' films, where the breed is shown in his role as the Carriage Dog. However, the most well-known film depicting the breed is Walt Disney's *101 Dalmatians*. The original book was written by Dodie Smith, who owned the breed, and was a member of the British Dalmatian Club for many years.

Having watched the film on more than one occasion, I feel certain that the people who did the animation for *101 Dalmatians* must have spent many hours studying the breed, for their reproduction of expressions and mannerisms are so true to life. I am sure that anybody who owns a Dalmatian can see their own dog on the screen, at some point during the film.

DALMATIAN CHARACTERISTICS

A Dalmatian is a lovely dog to look at with his spectacular markings of black or liver spots against a pure-white background. The breed's temperament is also distinctive, as anyone who has owned the breed will testify. Typically, the Dalmatian is out-going and friendly. He should not be nervous or aggressive, but he should be quite capable of defending and protecting his family and home.

The Dalmatian is a very loyal companion and will return all the love you can give him, and probably more besides. These dogs like human company and enjoy being part of a family. They are full of life and fun, but are capable of adapting to suit most lifestyles, be it slow and sedate, or fast and hectic.

Although not the easiest breed to train, with patience they can be trained for many tasks, even adapting back to their old-time role of a hunting dog working with a gun. As a breed they are very intelligent, and if faced with a problem, most Dalmatians can normally work out an answer, usually to their own advantage!

This is a breed that likes exercise. In fact, it is hard to tire an adult Dalmatian – you may be on your knees, but after few minutes rest your dog will be ready to go again. Bear in mind that a Carriage Dog would have been expected to travel fifteen to twenty miles a day, each day, keeping up with the horses. However, the Dalmatian also likes his creature comforts, and will be quick to claim his place snoozing in front of the fire.

It sounds as though the Dalmatian is the perfect pet for everybody, but this is not always the case. Dalmatians can be very strong-minded and will do what you want them to do, only as long as it suits them. They need a lot of patience while training, and very firm handling when they are young, especially the 'teenage' males (one to two years of age). You always need to be one step ahead in thought – if you are not,

It became a mark of high fashion to have a pair of Dalmatians running behind the family carriage.

It appears that Dalmatians of today still retain an affinity with horses.

Males are larger and stronger than females, and they sometimes have a stronger personality.

The liver-spotted Dalmatian is just as attractive as the black-spotted, but there are not so many of them. If you choose a bitch, remember that you will have to cope with her seasonal cycle.

then you risk the dog becoming your pack leader. A Dalmatian is a far stronger dog than most people realise. The friendly, spotted dog actually camouflages a lot of weight and muscle. Physically, young children are not capable of controlling one of the breed on a lead and should never be allowed to take them for walks unaccompanied.

OWNING A DALMATIAN

Taking on a dog – no matter which breed – is a commitment that must last for the duration of your pet's life. You should not be tempted to buy a puppy without first thinking about the disadvantages of owning one. If you have doubts, then take more time to think about the responsibilities of owning a dog in an ever-changing society, which has a forceful anti-dog faction.

On average, a Dalmatian lives in the region of eleven or twelve years, though the breed can easily live into their mid-to-late teens. Therefore, this means ten or more years of owning a dog full of life and still capable of a lot of vigorous exercise. Even in their later years Dalmatians do not, like some other breeds, become slow and sedate with the passing of time. Before you decide to take on this commitment, you should ask yourself the following questions.

1. Can you afford to own a medium-sized, active dog?

The expense does not end with the purchase price. You will have to pay vet's fees, feeding bills, plus buying items of equipment such as a lead, collar, a bed and grooming equipment.

2. Do you have the space?

You must be able to accommodate your Dalmatian comfortably in the house, as well as having a securely-fenced garden of a suitable size.

3. Do you have the time and energy to spend with your Dalmatian?

Your dog will need part of your time each day to attend to his feeding, grooming and exercising – not just in the first few weeks and months, but for the rest of his life.

4. Is there a member of your family at home for most of each day?

Dalmatians are not a suitable breed to be left on their own, for eight hours a day, five days a week, while the 'family' goes out to work. If left for long periods on a regular basis, your Dalmatian will become bored, and a bored Dalmatian invariably becomes destructive.

5. Does the person who spends most time at home really want a dog?

Inevitably, this is the person who will feed, groom and exercise the dog, and so you must be confident that this arrangement will work, each and every day.

This list of questions may appear daunting, but it is far better to think carefully before rushing out and buying the first Dalmatian you come across. Owning a dog is one of the most rewarding experiences, and if, after due consideration, you and your family are confident that you can provide a suitable home, I can assure you it is a decision you will never regret.

FINDING A BREEDER

It is essential to make a good start to your dog-owning life, and so your first task is to locate a responsible breeder who has some nice, healthy Dalmatians for sale. Your national Kennel Club will supply a list of Breed Club secretaries, and they will in turn give you names of breeders in your area for you to contact. The secretary may be able to tell you which breeders have puppies available.

Before you make an appointment to visit a breeder, there are a number of decisions to make:

MALE OR FEMALE?

This really comes down to personal choice, but there are some practical differences between the two which may need to be discussed.

1. Males are normally larger than bitches, which, of course, also means that they are considerably heavier and stronger.

2. Males sometimes have stronger personalities than bitches, which can make them a little more difficult to control.

3. Bitches, if left un-neutered, will come into season at regular intervals throughout their life. The frequency of seasons varies from bitch to bitch. It can be approximately every six or seven months, or it can be at intervals considerably longer than that. During their season, which lasts approximately twenty-one days, most bitches will keep themselves clean, though there will be some staining of the bedding. During the part of the season when the bitch would be receptive to a male – this is for two or three days about the middle of the season – care must be taken to ensure that no accidental mating can take place. The bitch must not be allowed to roam, nor must any dogs be allowed access to her.

If it is not your intention to breed from your bitch, then she can be spayed (neutered) after her first season. Seasons can also be controlled by injections or tablets. Ask your vet for advice.

4. If you already have a dog and are thinking of getting a second, then it is usually better to consider one of the opposite sex and have one or both neutered. Two of the same sex can lead to problems if they start to argue for the top position, as the puppy gets older.

TWO PUPPIES?

However tempting it may seem to buy two puppies as company for each other, or for any other reason, please think twice about such a decision. Apart from the reasons against two of one sex, the main problem is training. *It is almost impossible to train two puppies at the same time.* A puppy needs individual attention, and while you are training one, the other gets into mischief. If you want two Dalmatians as company, buy one and when that one is reasonably trained and well-behaved (possibly at about 12-18 months), then buy your second puppy. By this time, the older dog will help to train your new puppy.

At six weeks of age, the puppies have their spots, but more are likely to appear over the next few months.

Chapter Two

CHOOSING A DALMATIAN

VISITING A BREEDER

When you have located some Dalmatian breeders in your area, make contact with a couple of them – not necessarily the one living nearest to you, or the one with puppies ready for sale immediately – and discuss the possibility of buying a puppy. Tell the breeder just what you are looking for: whether you want a male or female, whether you want black or liver-spotted, whether you require a potential show dog or pet (See Chapter 6: The Show Ring), and whether it is your intention in the future to breed a litter.

Dalmatians are not a highly commercial breed despite their good press and fanciability, and most of the genuine lovers of the breed do not over-breed. Litters can therefore be fully booked either before or very soon after the puppies are born. Many of the top Dalmatian breeders have a waiting list for their puppies, and so the

Ask the breeder if you can see the puppies' mother. She should be friendly and out-going, indicating that her puppies will be of equally sound temperament.

puppy of your choice may not be easily available.

Take your time and, if possible, see more than one litter while you are deciding what to do. All puppies are appealing, whatever their breed, so make sure that your head rules your heart, as it is a very important decision that you are about to make.

Most responsible breeders will also want to make sure that you and your home are suitable to own one of their puppies, so expect a lot of searching questions before you are accepted on to a waiting list. Do not take offence at these questions; they come from a deep love of the breed and the breeder's desire to ensure a lifetime home for their puppies. You will probably find that the breeder takes a lifelong interest in your puppy, and will be ready to offer help and advice at whatever stage it is requested. For preference, buy your puppy from somebody genuinely interested in the breed, rather than from a large commercial kennel with many different breeds for sale. Dalmatians are really not a breed to be bought from such places, however well run they appear to be.

The best time to buy a puppy is in spring, when, hopefully, you have all the good weather of summer ahead for the early training of your new family member. Unfortunately, puppies do not always arrive at the best time, so do be prepared to wait to buy the puppy you want.

ASSESSING THE LITTER

If you are buying a Dalmatian for the first time, by all means go to see the litter while the puppies are very young *if* the breeder agrees. You will find out what a litter of Dalmatians looks like, but there is not much point in trying to choose a puppy before it is at least six weeks old, as they change so much before that point. You should certainly not consider taking a puppy home before it is at least seven to eight weeks of age.

Try to arrange your visit or visits to see the litter at a time when the puppies will be most active. Do not arrive just after the puppies have been fed, as all they will want to do is to go to sleep. The general things to note when you visit the litter are the same whether the litter is in a kennel or in the house. The condition and future health of your puppy depends much on the care it receives in the first few weeks after birth.

Puppies are not easy to control, especially if the litter is large in number, and therefore they will probably be contained, either in a whelping box or exercise area.This area should be generally clean, dry, and away from draughts. The bedding area should also be clean. The puppies should look, and smell, clean and healthy, and they will usually be very lively. If, when you first arrive, the puppies are asleep, they should be all spread about the sleeping area, not piled in a heap. This indicates they are warm and content, rather than nestling together for warmth.

The best puppies to consider are the ones that come to you, bright-eyed and tails wagging. No matter how appealing you find the little pup backing off into a corner, do not buy it. All Dalmatian puppies should be friendly and interested in humans, and the shy, nervous puppy may have an unsound temperament. Frequently, one puppy will appear to 'choose' you. If you like the look of that puppy, then that is the one to buy.

At times the puppies may appear to be fighting. This is not normally a sign that they will be aggressive as they grow older, but the usual behaviour of a litter as they decide among themselves – even at such a young age – who is going to be the dominant puppy in the litter. All animals in a group have to determine a pecking order. In other words, somebody has to be the boss and the remainder are in order below. It is worth remembering that the boss puppy is always going to be the one with the strongest personality.

Make sure that when you go to see puppies, you see the mother of the litter. She will be a better guide to the future temperament of your chosen puppy. Hopefully, she will be happy to greet you, full of fun and eager to show off her puppies. If when you first see her, especially in the first two or three weeks after the birth, she appears protective towards her litter, this is quite normal.

By the time the puppies are about five weeks old and becoming a little less dependent on her, she should return to her usual behaviour. If she shows nervousness or aggression towards you, then it is possible that she will have taught her pups that behaviour pattern towards humans. This could be difficult to overcome in the future, although with patience and time it can usually be reversed. It is not always possible to see the sire of the litter, without making another journey elsewhere. Many breeders do not own the stud dog they have used, preferring to use a male owned by another person. As a guide to the future, it can be worthwhile making the effort to travel to see the sire, especially if you are buying a male puppy.

THE RIGHT CHOICE

As a general guide when looking at a litter of Dalmatians, remember that at six or seven weeks of age they probably will not have all their spots. New ones appear for several months, so a puppy with a lot of spots and not much white at six weeks, will look even spottier when it is an adult. If, when you look at a puppy, there is something about its appearance that you don't like, such as too many spots, or a black ear, or a blue eye, then don't buy it. As the puppy becomes older, that part of its appearance will only seem to get worse, and irritate you every time you look at it.

Do not buy any puppy that you are not really sure about, whatever the temptations may be to do so. Remember you have got to live with and love that dog for many years to come!

It does not follow that the smallest or largest puppy in the litter will always be small or large. Once puppies leave the litter, they can alter immensely, and the adult size of your puppy can depend upon many different factors. Finding the right puppy is probably not as easy as you thought it would be, but it is important to persevere until you are confident in your choice.

A WORD OF WARNING

Dalmatians do have a problem, which has always been acknowledged by breeders, and that is a predisposition to inherited deafness. (See Chapter 7: Breeding Dalmatians). Hearing Assessment Testing of puppies can be undertaken by the breeder on a BAER machine, before they are of a age to sell, and each puppy so tested will receive a certificate to declare the hearing status of that puppy. If at all possible, you should buy a puppy that has been tested for hearing, especially if you are considering breeding from the puppy in the future. *Do not buy a deaf puppy, however appealing it may be.*

NAMING YOUR PUPPY

Once you have chosen your puppy, decide upon the name you are going to call him

This is a fit and healthy puppy, but he is lacking in spots and has a blue eye. He still has the makings of a first-class pet, but you should be aware of physical 'faults' which will not change with maturity.

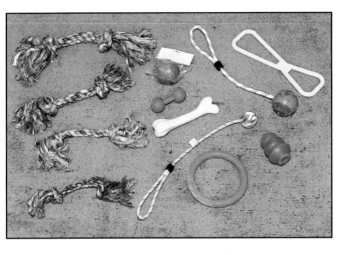

If you are buying toys for your Dalmatian, make sure they are made of materials he cannot easily chew.

There are many different types of feeding bowls on the market. The stainless steel type is the most suitable for a Dalmatian.

or her at home. This should be a name that is easy to call when the dog is out for exercise – imagine how it will sound if you are calling the name in a crowded place. It is easier to use a name containing two syllables, such as 'Amber', 'Susie' or 'Major', rather than a single syllable such as 'Jet'. Try to suit the name to the puppy; he will have to live with it for many years, and so will you. Once you have chosen a name, ask the breeder to use that name when talking to your puppy. In that way, your pup will be used to his name, and he will hopefully be more responsive when you take him home.

It is also a good idea to give the breeder a piece of bedding that can be used by the litter the day before you are collecting your own puppy. Take this home with you and use it in your puppy's bed, so he will have familiar smells around him as a comfort when he is on his own for the first time.

PREPARATIONS
There is a fair amount to do before you bring your puppy home, planning where the new arrival is going to sleep, what is it going to eat, and what equipment you will need. It is far better to make all the necessary arrangements beforehand, rather than being unprepared when you try to settle your Dalmatian puppy into his new home.

LIVING QUARTERS
Dalmatians can live outside in kennels, provided the kennel is well built, waterproof, damp-proof, and free from draughts. A small wooden kennel is not really suitable; a structure made of brick, blocks or something similar would be better. Ideally, it should be large enough for you to walk into, so you can clean it thoroughly inside. The bed needs to be raised off the floor, with adequate bedding, depending on the outside temperature and bearing in mind that Dalmatians do not have a long coat. The doorway should not face the direction of the prevailing wind, otherwise the dog will be most uncomfortable.

A Dalmatian can adapt perfectly well to outside accommodation, but there is no doubt that Dalmatians do prefer to live indoors. After all, if you are keeping your dog as a pet, it is far better if lives as part of the family. If you opt for keeping your Dalmatian in the house, you will need to decide where the puppy is going to sleep. The area should be dry and free from draughts, and there should be enough space for a fully-grown Dalmatian to lie out comfortably. It is important that once you have chosen a place, it will always be the 'dog's space'. Every dog needs somewhere to call his own – a place to retreat to when he (or you) wants some peace and quiet.

BEDS AND CRATES
While the puppy is small, it is probably better to use a sturdy cardboard box (without any metal staples in it), as a bed. Cut one side down lower to make a 'door', giving the puppy easy access. The puppy will feel far more secure in a smaller box rather than a full-sized dog bed, and the size of box can be increased as the weeks go by, until the puppy is a large enough to need a proper bed.

The choice of a dog bed can be difficult – there are many different types, but some are really not suitable for a Dalmatian, unless you are prepared to keep renewing the bed. Wicker baskets and soft materials (such as beanbags) are easily chewed. The kidney-shaped plastic dog beds are far more practical, though even these can become a little chewed around the edge. The size of bed for an adult

Dalmatian needs to be large enough for the dog to sleep in with comfort, and therefore needs to be a minimum of 27-30 inches across.

You can consider buying a dog crate – indeed, this is a standard item of equipment in America. It is extremely useful and practical, provided the dog is encouraged to regard the crate as 'his place', going there out of choice when the door is left open, and only confined in it for short periods. It is essential that the crate is large enough for the *adult* dog to stand, turn and lie down in comfort. It will obviously look far too large for your puppy.

However, if the puppy is trained to sleep in his crate from an early age, it will last him most, if not all, of his life. Some crates are made of a heavy duty welded-mesh and are fully collapsible. They are made in many different sizes and shapes (and qualities), with the door either at the end, or at the side, with others being designed to fit into individual types of cars. The benefits of crates are many and varied. The plus-points are:

1. The crate is collapsible, so it can be used in the car, making travel with your dog much safer. The dog is contained and cannot escape if the car door is opened for any reason.
2. Travel away from home is much easier, as the dog always has his own space yet is secure while in a strange place. Many hotels will not allow dogs loose in their rooms but will allow dogs in crates.
3. If your dog is unfortunate enough to injure himself and rest is essential to quick/complete recovery, then the crate provides a comfortable place for his enforced rest.
4. There will be occasions when you have visitors at home and the company of a dog is not suitable. In this situation, your dog will be quite happy in his crate.

The crates normally include a removable plastic tray in the base. I find these a little slippery for a Dalmatian, and I prefer to use a piece of carpet (not rubber-backed) cut to size, with bedding on top.

BEDDING
Your Dalmatian will need a good supply of bedding – no dog should sleep on a bare bed. The choice of bedding needs to be of a type that can either be washed frequently, such as cotton sheeting, woollen blankets or the special fleecy type of dog bedding. You can use bedding that can easily be renewed, such as shredded paper, but this can get rather messy for a dog in the house.

FEEDING BOWLS
There are many types of dog bowls on the market, both for food and water, and without a doubt, stainless-steel is the best for a Dalmatian. Plastic bowls get chewed in a very short time; the ceramic/pottery bowls will be picked up by the dog and dropped, usually on a hard surface; aluminium bowls discolour the dog's teeth.

Before you bring your puppy home, make sure you have a supply of the food he is used to. The breeder should supply you with a diet sheet, and it is advisable to ask for this before you collect your puppy. It is important to keep on the same diet, at least to begin with, rather than introducing a change during the stressful settling-in period. The breeder may give you some food for the puppy to cover the first few meals, but it is better to be safe than find yourself without the right food.

Dalmatians are ideal pets to have in a family with young children, but do not let your puppy become overwhelmed by meeting too many people when he first arrives home.

TOYS

If you intend to buy toys for your puppy, make sure that they are made of materials that he cannot easily chew, and that they are not too small or he could choke on them, as even small puppy teeth can be very destructive. Hard rubber or plastic balls (about tennis-ball size or larger) or bone-shaped toys are suitable. Squeaky toys can amuse some youngsters, but make sure the puppy does not chew around the squeaker and swallow it. Wooden toys are not really advisable, as the dog may get splinters in his mouth

Beware of giving your puppy an old slipper to play with – he will not realise that your 'new' slippers are not his playthings. One cheap idea is to take a piece of old denim or similar hard-wearing material (the leg of an old pair of jeans, for example) roll it up and then tie a large knot in the centre – this will keep a puppy amused for hours. The same applies to a length of very thick, knotted rope or the manufactured cotton raggers – both are virtually indestructible.

THE VET

It is advisable to make contact with a vet (preferably one that is recommended by your puppy's breeder or other dog-owners in your neighbourhood) before you bring your puppy home, just in case you are faced with an emergency straight away and do not know anyone locally.

Chapter Three

CARING FOR YOUR PUPPY

COLLECTING YOUR PUPPY

Hopefully, you will not be travelling too far to collect your puppy, but whatever the distance, try to make the trip as early in the day as possible so that your puppy has time to settle into his new home before bedtime. You will need to take the following with you to make the journey easier:

1. Newspapers and/or absorbent paper to clean any mess the puppy may make.
2. One or more large towels – the puppy may drool or be sick.
3. A plastic bag in which to put any rubbish.
4. A bowl and a bottle of water. This is only necessary if you have a long journey or the weather is hot.

It is easier if two people travel to bring the puppy home so that the passenger can tend to the puppy, if necessary, during the journey. Do not take a crowd of people,

The first night can be traumatic for a new puppy as he will miss the warmth and comfort of his littermates

especially young children. This will be the most stressful time that the puppy will have had during his short life, and everything should be done to make it as easy as possible. When you arrange to collect your puppy from the breeder, make sure the puppy has not just been fed, as this will increase the chance of travel sickness.

Some new owners prefer the puppy to travel on the passenger's knee on a towel or blanket, in order to give reassurance during the journey. If you have an estate car, station wagon or hatchback, you may prefer the puppy to travel at the rear, but bear in mind that a puppy, loose in such a comparatively large area, is going to feel very insecure, and is liable to be thrown from side to side if the road is not reasonably straight. If the puppy is to be loose at the rear of the car, there should be sufficient soft bedding for the puppy to snuggle into, and make sure there is nothing movable at the back which could roll and possibly hurt the puppy. Do not allow the puppy to be loose on the seats, he could fall and hurt himself badly. All these are good reasons for using a crate.

If the journey is lengthy and the puppy likely to want to relieve himself during that time, it would be advisable to take as large a cardboard box as possible, lined in the base with papers, in which the puppy can be placed to empty himself. The puppy should not be placed directly on the ground in a strange place, because, at this stage, he could catch infections left by other dogs.

ARRIVING HOME

It is most important when you arrive home that your puppy is not overwhelmed by a large number of people, especially excited children. He will probably want to empty his bladder after the stress of the journey, in which case take him somewhere quiet, either outside in the garden or inside on papers, and let him relieve himself. Offer some water or a small amount of milk in case he is thirsty, but do not attempt to feed him at this point.

Your puppy will be most bewildered and confused by all that has happened. He has been taken from his home, family and everything that has meant security for the past few weeks, and now finds himself in strange surroundings with people he does not know. It is possible that his first instinct will be to run and hide. If he does, leave him for a while, he will probably re-emerge as he realises there is no danger. Puppies are incredibly inquisitive, and your pup will soon start to wander about the room.

At first he may appear to be hesitant, possibly almost crawling around rather than walking properly. Do not worry about this, it is perfectly normal. Your puppy will soon gain confidence, and return to his normal demeanour. Allow him to get to this stage as quietly as possible – too much noise and too many people will frighten him. Once your puppy appears confident let him follow you around into the other rooms. Do not rush him – with each new experience and place, let him take it at his own pace. Make sure during this time that your puppy is made familiar with his new bed and its surroundings.

INTRODUCING THE FAMILY

Young children find it difficult to understand the needs of a very young puppy, therefore, however disappointing it may seem, try to arrange the arrival of your puppy when the children will be out for a while. In this way, your puppy will have had a chance to settle in before the excitement of meeting new people. Remember that a human must appear very large to a young puppy, therefore it is better, to start with, if you come down to his size. When you are encouraging your puppy to come to you, crouch down so that you do not appear as large.

If you already have an older dog, take care with their initial introduction and you probably will not encounter much of a problem. The best way is to allow the puppy to settle into his new surroundings for a while, before letting the older dog in to see the new arrival. It is best to put your older dog on to a lead to introduce them, in order to have some control over what happens. Allow them to meet naturally – do not force them together – and try not to give the older dog any cause to be jealous of the puppy. As far as the older dog is concerned, the puppy is an intruder.

Provided that the older dog does not attack the puppy in a manner likely to cause serious damage, there can be grumbles and growls from the older dog, and he may even roll the puppy on to its back. This is nothing to panic about, the older dog is merely emphasising that he is the boss and the puppy must do as he is told. Most times the introduction will be licks and sniffing, before developing into a game. Sometimes the adult will take a strong objection to the 'intruder'. If this happens, separate the pair and make sure that the older dog knows that you will not tolerate such behaviour. Re-introduce the two, but make sure they are closely supervised until the older dog realises that the puppy poses no threat to him or the household. Strange as it may seem, some older dogs can be afraid of puppies.

Occasionally, the adult dog will object to the newcomer in a totally different manner, refusing to acknowledge that the puppy even exists, let alone is living in the same household. In these cases, after the initial meeting, the older dog will ignore the puppy, sometimes leaving the room when the puppy enters, or turning his back to the puppy and not even looking at it. This can last for several days – one of my own dogs behaved in this manner for three weeks before he accepted that the puppy was there to stay – but after that they were the best of friends.

THE FIRST MEAL

Your puppy may have missed a meal because of changing homes, but this will not do him any harm. When his first meal at your house is due, do not be tempted to give him a double amount to compensate for any meals missed, as this will only upset his stomach. Feed the normal meal and quantity suggested by the breeder on the diet sheet.

It is important to establish where your puppy is going to be fed, and from then onwards, always feed him in that area. Make sure your puppy is not disturbed while he is eating. Your puppy may refuse to eat, but this not a cause for concern – he will still be feeling strange and possibly a little homesick. By the next meal time he will probably be back to his normal appetite. Make sure there is a plentiful supply of clean and fresh cold water available for the dog to drink if he wants, irrespective of any other drinks he may be given, especially in hot weather.

THE FIRST NIGHT

By this time you should have decided where your new arrival is going to sleep, and he should already have been introduced to his bed. If you have left a blanket or a piece of bedding at the breeder's kennels, and then collected it with your puppy, you will find that the puppy will settle better snuggled up with something that smells familiar.

Do not worry if your puppy does not eat his first meal after arriving home – he will make up for it at the next mealtime.

The Dalmatian has much to learn. This youngster has learnt to tolerate the collar and lead, although he has yet to learn more formal obedience.

Most Dalmatians enjoy car travel. It is helpful if you have a dog cage or a crate in your car so your dog has somewhere safe and secure to settle.

The first night can be very traumatic for your puppy. It will probably be his first night alone, and he will miss the warmth and company of the other puppies. To overcome this problem there are several things that you can try:

1. Place a hot-water bottle (not too hot) in the bottom of your puppy's box, ensuring that it is securely wrapped so that he cannot chew it, with his blanket on top. This will provide the warmth and smell of the other pups.
2. It is said that a clock placed next to the bed will help to soothe a puppy, as the ticking will remind him of his mother's heartbeat.
3. A radio left playing quietly for a few nights may help to make the puppy feel less alone.

It is quite possible that the puppy will cry, howl or bark, either when you put him to bed or during the night. This is quite usual and very understandable, as he will be feeling very lonely and deserted. If your puppy appears to be getting very distressed, then it is advisable to go to him, give him a lot of reassurance and possibly a small drink of milk, then put him back to bed. Try not to do this too often, and certainly not after the first few nights, or it will develop into a habit with the puppy.

I would not advise you to move the puppy into your own room as a way of keeping him quiet, unless you want him always to sleep there. This night-time crying should only last a few nights at the most – just until the puppy has settled into his new home and routine.

CHILDREN AND DALMATIANS
Young children must be taught the importance of the correct behaviour towards a new puppy – *a puppy is not a new toy!*

Children must learn not to disturb the dog when he is asleep, especially while the puppy is young (and during old age, when a dog is not quite so tolerant). Teasing must not be allowed – no matter the age of the dog. Sooner or later the dog will object and possibly retaliate by biting. Obviously, children must never ill-treat the dog, however unintentionally.

The dog must be taught how to behave with children, learning not take advantage by begging for food, stealing food, jumping up, or any other anti-social behaviour. Although children will want to take the dog out for walks, this should not be allowed, unless accompanied by an adult.

Dalmatians and children make a very fine partnership, provided they are both taught how to behave together. Please do not let the situation arise where either one hurts the other.

THE FIRST FEW WEEKS

FEEDING
It is important to establish a feeding routine that suits both the puppy and the household. This should be established from a young age, and should be adhered to – with minimum disruption – throughout your dog's life.

Assuming your puppy is seven or eight weeks old, he will be needing four meals a day: two milk meals and two meat meals. Obviously as he gets older, this will change. A growing dog will require larger quantities, but a smaller number of meals.

While exact quantities cannot be laid down because each puppy has his own requirements, I have found the following routine fits most families and requires little changing:

WEANING TO SIXTEEN WEEKS
(Four meals a day.)

BREAKFAST AND TEA: I prefer these to be the meat meals, so when the number of meals is reduced these meals do not have to be changed. They should consist of either:-
1. Soaked, plain puppy-meal, mixed with a good-quality finely chopped (minced) meat, either raw or cooked.
2. A commercial complete puppy feed. These are widely available in either canned or dry form. If you feed dry food, soak it in hot water and leave to stand for about one hour prior to feeding. Follow the manufacturer's instructions as to quantity at first, but adjust, if necessary, to your own puppy's appetite.

LUNCH AND SUPPER: These will be the two milk meals, which will not be given as the puppy gets older. Each meal should consist of full-cream milk, adding one egg-yolk per pint, mixed with cereal, rice pudding, or porridge. A teaspoon of honey may be added to these meals.

If you are feeding a balanced diet using good-quality food, it should not be necessary for supplements to be given. This is especially important if a commercial puppy feed is used, as these are already balanced to meet a puppy's requirements. If you feel you must use a supplement then use a good-quality bone-flour or bonemeal that is produced for animal feed (not the type for use in the garden), and add a small amount to one meal once, or at most twice, a week.
Do not feed large amounts of any supplements, they can harm your puppy rather than do good. This applies particularly to cod-liver oil and calcium supplements.

FOUR TO SIX MONTHS
(Three meals a day.)
At this stage I find it the most convenient to stop the midday milk meal. The other three meals to remain as before, but a larger grade of biscuit-meal can be introduced as opposed to puppy-meal. If you are using a manufactured complete diet, be guided by the feeding instructions as to when you should change to the next grade.

FROM SIX MONTHS
(Two meals a day.)
The time has come to stop the evening milk meal, leaving the two meat meals. If supplements have been included in the diet, these should not be needed after this stage. A well-balanced diet should contain everything your dog needs.
I prefer to continue to feed two meals daily to all dogs over this age for several reasons:
1. If the dog has two equally-sized meals, it appears to lessen the chance of bloat occurring from an over-loaded stomach. (See Chapter 8: Health Care.)

2. The dog appears more contented and less likely to beg for food at your mealtimes.

3. If you need to alter the amount you are feeding (if your dog is overweight or underweight), it is easier to make two small alterations rather than one large one, and the dog does not appear to notice the change.

No two dogs require the same amount of food; each one differs and factors such as temperature, exercise, and temperament all make a difference to the amount required to keep a dog healthy. As the weeks pass and your puppy grows, he will obviously require more food. It is usually better to increase the amount in the two meat meals, as these are the two meals he will continue to be fed, and leave the milk meals without much of an increase.

If your puppy always leaves food in his dish you are probably giving him too much. If he continues to search for food after being fed, he probably needs a little more. Ideally, a puppy should clean his bowl at each meal. *Remember that clean water should always be available, whatever you feed your puppy.*

Puppies should not be given too many, if any, tidbits, especially sweets and biscuits etc. A dog is better with a controlled diet, and will be less likely to develop digestive problems and form bad habits.

HOUSE-TRAINING

Dalmatians are, on the whole, a very clean breed and they are usually easy to house-train. However, this training cannot be rushed, and it does require a fair amount of discipline on the part of the owner. When your puppy first arrives home, it is important to bear in mind that the pup does not know he is doing wrong if he makes any mess on your carpet or floor. His instinct tells him not to soil his bed – but that is the extent of his knowledge. You have to teach him that, in effect, all your house is his bed.

A small puppy does not have a large capacity in his bladder, and during the day he will need to empty himself at quite frequent intervals. When the puppy is asleep, especially at night, the bladder does not need to be emptied as frequently. Start the training by taking your puppy outside into the garden as soon as he wakes from a sleep, as soon as he has had a meal or drink, and at intervals in between, especially if he starts to squat or looks as though he is sniffing and circling, searching for somewhere to go.

If you have a special place in the garden that you want to use as a toilet area, take your puppy to that place each time. The most important part of the training is that you stay with the puppy, encouraging him with remarks such as "quickly", "hurry up", or "be good". At first the puppy will not understand, but he will gradually realise the connection between your words and what he is to do. When he 'performs', give him plenty of praise. Young puppies usually empty their bowels reasonably soon after a meal. If you put your puppy out on his own, all he will do is try to get back inside or explore the garden – he will not know what is expected of him. So, whatever the weather, you must stay outside with your puppy and be patient, for he will not always perform immediately.

Never shout at or chastise your puppy if he has made a mess in the house. A puppy is not capable of understanding that he is being punished for something he did earlier. If you catch him in the act, tell him "No" in a very stern voice, and quickly carry him outside.

Socialisation is a vital part of early training. This Dalmatian has been taught from puppyhood to accept the household cats.

The well-socialised dog takes all new experiences in his stride.

If you have decided to use a crate for your puppy, house-training can be made a little easier, as the pup will be reluctant to make a mess in his sleeping area. At night or when you leave your puppy for any length of time, place his bed in one half of the crate, with paper at the other end for him to use. During the day a young puppy should not be confined for long periods – thirty to forty-five minutes is the most at any one time – and then the puppy should be taken outside immediately to relieve himself. The pup will get very distressed if he is confined for longer periods because he will be forced to soil his bed, through no fault of his own.

Most breeders use newspapers spread on the floor around the sleeping area of their litters to make it easier to clean up after the puppies. Therefore, because the puppies are normally used to 'going' on papers, if you place papers on the floor by your door the puppy will usually go there to empty himself rather than other places. As the puppy gets older and more able to control himself, make the area of paper smaller and finally move it outside.

Although puppies do not need to relieve themselves as frequently at night when sleeping, at first it will not be possible for your puppy to go through the night without emptying his bladder or possibly his bowels. As the puppy grows, so will his ability to stay dry, so be patient if you find a mess in the morning. If possible, when you wake in the morning, make it your first priority to take the puppy outside.

This all might sound very complicated, but if you get into a routine of taking your puppy outside and watching him very carefully when he is inside, you can normally complete basic house training with a Dalmatian puppy in a week or two (some do take longer). After that, you will still have the odd accident during the day, but usually that is because the puppy could not get out, or you did not notice the puppy asking to go out. Vigilance is the keyword for the first few weeks.

If you already have an older dog, you will find that most of the time your puppy will follow the 'oldie' outside and will soon learn what to do. However, there are occasions when the 'oldie' will decide: "If the puppy can relieve himself inside, then so can I". If this happens, be very firm with the older dog, and make him realise that such behaviour is not acceptable.

VACCINATIONS

For the first few weeks of their life, puppies are protected from many canine diseases by their maternal antibodies. These are provided by the mother before birth and shortly after birth in the milk. Most of this protection has been outgrown by the time the puppy is two to three months old, therefore the protection needs replacing by vaccination.

Discuss the vaccination programme with your vet, as he will know which diseases provide the most risk in your area, and he will also know at what stage the puppy should receive his inoculations. The major diseases to protect against are Distemper, Hepatitis, Leptospirosis and Parvovirus. The initial inoculations are usually given at around ten weeks, followed by a second inoculation two weeks later. It then takes about ten days for the protective antibodies to build to the required strength.

Until your puppy has received this protection, it is unwise to expose him to any risk of infection. Therefore, you should only let him run in your own garden, or in places where you know that no other dogs have been recently. Do not be tempted to take your puppy out into public places until the vaccination programme has been completed.

Future boosters for these inoculations should be discussed with your vet – most advise an annual booster. If you intend to leave your dog in boarding kennels for any reason, you will probably find that an up-to-date vaccination certificate is required before the dog will be accepted.

SOCIALISATION

Although you cannot take your puppy out into the world before his inoculations are complete, you can still start the process of socialising your Dalmatian. Allow your puppy to greet and mix with visitors at home. Do not let strangers overpower him, but let him make the first approaches.

Introduce your puppy to various household appliances, such as the vacuum cleaner and washing machine, teaching him that machines and noise are nothing to be afraid of. Play the radio with different types of programmes – music, talk shows etc. – both loudly and quietly.

Take your puppy for rides in the car. They only need to be short journeys, just to get him used to travelling away from home and then to return. If you have friends or family who do not have a dog of their own, or have a dog that is fully vaccinated, you can introduce your puppy to new places. While your Dalmatian is still small enough to carry (that does not last for long), try and sit or stand by a busy road, taking care not to let him on to the ground or come into contact with other dogs. In this way, your puppy will get used to the sound and sight of traffic.

When you introduce your puppy to new situations, give him plenty of encouragement and petting, and show him he has nothing to fear. Try to introduce your puppy to as many new things as possible between the ages of seven and twelve weeks – this is an important stage in his life when he will be learning at a very rapid rate. Puppies that are isolated during this crucial period may show apprehension and fear at all new situations in later life.

Between the ages of eight to eleven weeks, care must be taken not to frighten the puppy, with sudden movements, loud noises or harsh handling, as any traumatic mental or physical events at this stage can have a long-lasting effect. Love and cuddles will help to overcome any traumas at this vulnerable time. For example, when you take your puppy to the vet for his first injection, make sure he is not frightened by the needle or by the vet himself. Give lots of praise and reassurance, possibly some tidbits, to help your puppy overcome his fear, or you may have a dog that is always afraid of going to the vet.

EXERCISE

It must be remembered that young puppies do not need and should not have too much exercise. Once your puppy is lead-trained, short walks on a lead are quite sufficient. As the puppy grows and his training becomes more reliable, the walks can be a little longer and some free-running can be introduced. Too much vigorous exercise on growing bones and joints can lead to future problems.

If you do not want to bath your dog, give him a quick rub-down with a towel and then leave him to dry in a warm place. The mud will then drop off his coat with only a light brushing.

Chapter Four

ADULT MANAGEMENT

DIET

Feeding the adult Dalmatian is a continuation of the regime for feeding your puppy, but by this point he will be on two meals daily, one in the morning and one in the evening, at times that suit your routine. It is best if you can feed at approximately the same time each day.

The type of diet is a matter of personal choice, but as with the puppy it can be either:

1. A meat and biscuit meal, using good-quality fresh or canned meat with biscuit-meal that has been soaked in hot water and allowed to cool.

2. A manufactured complete diet, either of the dry or canned variety.

Too much variation in the diet can lead to digestive problems. All changes should be introduced gradually over several days if you are to avoid upset stomachs. As with puppies, all adults are different, and need varying amounts of food. Therefore, the amount of food given will depend on your dog's individual needs.

The Dalmatian's coat is easy to care for, and a regular routine of bushing once or twice a week will keep your dog in top-class condition.

As a general guide for weight, feel the ribs on your dog. For normal weight, you should just be able to feel the ribs under your fingers. If your dog is overweight, you will not be able to feel the ribs properly, but will have to press through a layer of fat to feel them. If your dog is underweight, you will be able to see his ribs from across the room.

Regulate the amount of food your dog has to eat, so that he is just nicely covered, neither underweight and definitely not overweight, as the latter can seriously affect his overall health. Increase or decrease both daily meals by small amounts to keep the weight correct – your dog probably will not even notice the difference.

GROOMING

For most of the year a Dalmatian coat is easy to look after. All that is needed is a regular brushing with a bristle brush, once or twice a week, followed by a wipe-over with a damp chamois leather or cloth. Unfortunately, when your Dalmatian goes into his twice-yearly moult, the white hairs appear to multiply in number at a very rapid rate, especially on the carpet! At this time your dog will need brushing at least once a day, (preferably outside, and not when you are wearing black!). A rubber grooming glove, available from most pet shops, or a small rubber curry comb, should be used in addition to the bristle brush.

BATHING

Unless your dog has found himself a nice 'smell' to roll in – which will make a bath very necessary – a well-groomed Dalmatian will not need frequent bathing. A bath once or twice a year should be sufficient. If you bath your dog, use a mild shampoo, making sure that the coat is thoroughly rinsed off. Towel your dog dry to remove all excess water, ensuring that he is kept warm until he is thoroughly dry. If possible, train your dog to sit so you can dry him with a hair-dryer.

In wet weather, you may find that your dog is covered with mud splashes when he returns from exercise. At times like this it is best to rub the dog down with an old towel, then leave him in a warm place for a short while, and as he dries the mud will normally drop from his coat with only a light brushing.

Frequent bathing results in the loss of natural oils from the coat, and as a result, dirt will cling to the coat even more easily. A well-balanced diet will help to keep your dog's coat in good condition, and naturally oiled.

TEETH

Keeping your dog's teeth clean is not always easy, especially if the diet is mainly of soft food. A few hard dog biscuits, given each week, will help to keep the teeth clean. Bones are also excellent for this purpose, but *only* the correct type of bone. The only bone that is suitable for a Dalmatian is either a large beef knuckle or marrow bone (thigh bone). These can either be fresh bones from the butcher, or prepared/sterilised bones, available from pet shops. Small bones (such as lamb bones) or soft bones (such as rib bones) are not suitable. They can lead to problems if they splinter and can cause a blockage in the intestines. Dalmatians must never be given bones from any kind of poultry or fish.

There are products available, such as toothpaste specifically made for dogs, and it is possible to train your puppy, once his adult teeth have grown, to allow you to clean his teeth, as you would your own. You may find that your dog's teeth start to become covered in tartar. If this becomes too severe, your dog's breath become very smelly, and the teeth and gums will become infected. Tartar can be removed using a tooth-scaler, or you can arrange regular dental check-ups with your vet.

FEET AND NAILS
Good foot care is important whether you live in the town or in the country, and a little care will prevent possible lameness.

Try making it your routine to inspect your dog's feet whenever you return from exercising him. It only takes a few seconds to check that there are no cuts on his pads (the areas without fur, under his feet), and that nothing is lodged between the pads or toes. If you have been walking in the street, it is important to check that your dog does not have any tar on his pads or small stones stuck between his pads, especially if the weather is very hot or there are any new road surfaces nearby. In the country, make sure that no thorns or seeds have penetrated the skin on the feet, as these can be very painful.

Some dogs have soft nails and these will wear naturally as the dog is exercised, but others can have very hard nails and these will probably need cutting or trimming to keep the feet in good condition. If nails are allowed to become too long, not only will they look unsightly and spoil the look of the foot, but they will start to hurt the dog as he walks, especially on hard surfaces.

The nails can be cut quite easily if you do this as a routine, starting within the first few weeks of obtaining your puppy. At first you will only need sharp scissors or ordinary nail-clippers, but as the puppy grows and his nails become harder, it is better to use the guillotine type of nail-clippers made for dogs. If the nails are trimmed regularly, you will only need to cut the tip of the nail. You must never cut back into the quick (the pink centre of the nail), as this will hurt the dog and the nail will bleed profusely. You will also have a dog who will be reluctant to have his nails clipped again in future.

If you are nervous about trimming the nails, or if your pup has all-black or liver nails, which makes it much more difficult to see the quick, then it is possible to keep the nails short by filing. For this, you need a medium-rough carpenter's file. It is best to hold the foot, and file from under the nail in an upwards direction, ensuring once again that you do not go back as far as the quick.

In extreme cases, if your dog refuses to have his nails trimmed, it may be necessary to arrange for your vet to do this work. This could be done at the same time as a dental check.

EXERCISE
Once your puppy approaches adult life, the amount of exercise can be increased. By the time your Dalmatian is over nine months of age, he will be able to cope with reasonably long walks, both on and off the lead. After about eighteen months, your dog will enjoy virtually unlimited exercise, and even the longest of walks will not really tire him. You may be weary, but after a short rest, your Dalmatian will be raring to go again.

To avoid problems associated with exercise it is best to bear the following in mind:
1. Do not exercise your dog too much in extremely hot weather, it is better to wait until a cooler part of the day.
2. If possible, do not let your dog jump from high places on to a solid surface, such

Feet should be inspected every time your dog returns from exercise. If the nails grow too long they will need to be trimmed, using the guillotine type of nail-clippers.

Check your Dalmatian's ears to ensure they are clean and smell fresh. If necessary, remove any excess wax with cotton-wool.

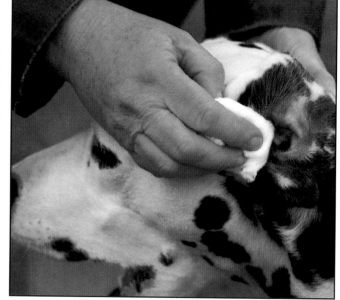

Gnawing a marrow bone is a good way to keep teeth clean, but your dog must never be left alone, unsupervised, with a bone.

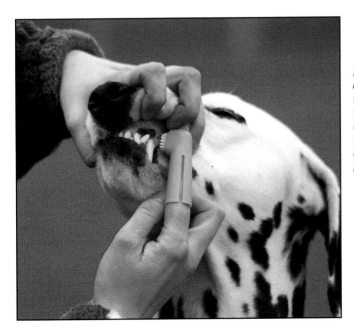

If tartar accumulates on the teeth, regular brushing with a toothbrush will soon solve the problem.

as concrete or loose stones – he could easily damage his feet or shoulders.

3. In very low temperatures, especially near water where ice has formed, make sure that your dog does not run on to thin ice.

4. Do not allow your dog to run loose near traffic.

5. Never allow your dog to run loose near livestock and poultry.

6. Always make sure your dog is under control, especially if there are children, other dogs, or elderly people around.

A well-controlled Dalmatian is a joy, not only to yourself but also to others, and you will find he soon gathers his own following of fans.

CAR JOURNEYS

Dalmatians, both young and old, normally enjoy riding in the car so it is very easy to train your dog to join you on your travels. If my 'old girl' managed to sneak into the car in a morning, there was no way that I could get her out again until teatime. A dog can be great company, when you are driving alone, and will normally guard the car whenever you have to leave it. However, there are a few points to remember if you travel with your dog, even if the journey is not very far:

1. If your dog is in the car for a long time, make sure he has a chance to relieve himself at regular intervals. Always take a supply of drinking water and bowl for your dog.

2. *Hot cars kill dogs within a very short time.* If you are travelling in very hot or sunny weather, make sure that there is shade in the car for the dog while you are on the move, and especially if you are in slow-moving traffic. Direct sun through the window can sometimes cause heatstroke.

On a hot or sunny day, never leave your dog in the car. Even if the weather is mild and you have parked in the shade, the temperature inside can rise incredibly quickly. This can be fatal for your dog. A dog cannot sweat to cool himself, like a human being, and so can very quickly overheat.

A thermometer kept in the car will show just how quickly the temperature soars. A car left in full sun with the windows open, will reach well over 100 degrees Fahrenheit (38 degrees Centigrade) within minutes, and can easily reach 150 degrees Fahrenheit (65 degrees Centigrade) – which would be fatal for your dog.

3. While hot cars are extremely dangerous, remember that, in winter, your car will become cold. If you leave the dog in the car in freezing or below freezing temperatures, make sure that he has sufficient bedding to keep him at a comfortable temperature.

Basically, if the inside of the car feels too hot, or too cold, for you to be comfortable, then your dog will be more severely affected.

THE OLDER DOG

Dalmatians, if well looked after, can lead a full and active life almost to the end. However, as your dog gets older he will need extra care. Old age to a Dalmatian, who has had good care all his life, usually starts from the age of ten onwards. It is important, therefore, that you take your dog's needs into account, and then you will have many happy years left together. Points to watch out for are:

1. Make sure that your dog does not get fat, especially as he gets older. Too much weight puts a strain on all the joints, on the heart, and makes exercise more difficult.

2. Reduce the amount of protein in the diet slightly as the dog reaches old age. A

number of complete diets are specifically made for the older dog.

3. Ensure that your dog is kept warm and dry, especially in cold weather and after exercise.

4. As your dog gets older, reduce the amount of hard exercise. Shorter and more frequent walks are better. It is important that you regulate how much exercise the dog has. Dalmatians seem to forget that they are getting older and want to carry on as they did in their youth. Do not let your dog get too tired and stiff.

EUTHANASIA

There will come a time, hopefully after many happy years of companionship, that the quality of life will not be as it should be for you and your Dalmatian. It is at this point that you may need to ask for your pet to be put to sleep, preferably at home in his own bed or chair, with you by his side. This is the one last act of kindness, and you owe it to the dog who has loved you and your family through all the ups and downs of life. However painful it may be for you, do not let him suffer.

The choke-chain is a useful aid, as long as it is only used in training sessions, and when your dog is walking at heel. The choke-chain must be fitted correctly, with the chain running through the top of the ring, which means that it releases automatically.

Chapter Five

TRAINING YOUR DALMATIAN

EARLY LESSONS
Training should really start from the moment you arrive home with your puppy. This should not be in any sort of formal manner, but rather by encouraging your puppy to do what you want, using your tone of voice and praising when he responds. As the weeks go by and your Dalmatian settles into your household, training can become a little more formal.

However, you must bear in mind that each step in training may take weeks or even months for the puppy to really learn. *Do not attempt to rush training.* Take it slowly, working for only a few minutes each day with a young puppy. If you attempt to do too much, the puppy will lose interest and become bored with the whole idea of pleasing you. The most important thing to remember when training or even just owning a Dalmatian is that "No" must mean "No"! You have got to be the boss, not the other way round, or you will never enjoy your relationship with your dog.

Hopefully, your puppy will be partially used to the sound of his name when you bring him home (see Chapter 3: Choosing a Puppy), but it is essential that you use the name frequently when talking to him in the early days to fully imprint the name on him.

Training does not just mean Obedience type of training, it also means learning to live with your dog in harmony. You have to teach your puppy what you consider acceptable behaviour and what you consider not acceptable. In your home, your puppy must learn to live by your rules.

TEACHING GOOD MANNERS

Your Dalmatian puppy is going to grow into quite a large-sized adult, and behaviour that looks cute at eight weeks can be totally unacceptable at eight months. I realise that my interpretation of acceptable may not be the same as yours, but the following behavioural problems have cropped up either in my own Dalmatians or other Dalmatians I have known. Like all bad habits, the sooner they are eliminated the better and, hopefully, you will find some of the suggestions of use when training your Dalmatian.

BITING
Every puppy will 'play-bite', and this should not be taken as bad temperament. You will find as you play with your puppy he will bite your hands, sleeves and anything else within reach of his mouth. This is perfectly natural; it is a continuation of the

play between littermates, when they were determining who was the 'boss'. However, it is important that you now assume the superior position. You must therefore stop the play-biting as quickly as possible, especially if you have young children. Whenever your puppy starts to bite, tell him "No" in a very stern voice. If the pup continues biting, tap him sharply on the nose with one or two fingers – he will soon realise that he must stop biting. If the puppy is playing with other people, especially children, you must make sure that his behaviour is under control at all times as puppy teeth are extremely sharp and can easily hurt. Do not let older children play too roughly with a young puppy as this will encourage play-biting.

CHEWING
Furniture and other household objects are often chewed by a young puppy, especially at the time he is changing from his puppy teeth to his adult teeth. As far as the puppy is concerned, the chair-leg is a convenient 'teething ring'. However, this habit must be eliminated at an early stage, as an adult that chews can cause an awful lot of damage in a very short time. Again, if you catch your puppy in the act of chewing, you must tell him "No", and if that does not work, follow it up with a swift tap on the nose. There is no point in telling your puppy off after he has chewed something, as he cannot relate the telling-off to an earlier event. All you can do is grit your teeth and keep a closer watch on him.

CLIMBING ON FURNITURE
Dalmatians love their comfort, and the best armchair or your bed will be most enticing. Some owners do not mind their pet sharing their armchair or their bed, but if you do not want your dog to do this, you must be firm right from the beginning. Your puppy will be quick to try his luck, and when you are sitting in your chair, it will be first his head on your knee or nose in your hand, then one paw will come to rest on your knee, then two front paws, then the whole of his front half will be resting across your knee, followed quietly by one back leg and then the other. Before you realise, your Dalmatian will be sitting on your knee looking very pleased with himself – and his thanks will be a large lick on your nose!

   In this situation it is hard to be tough, and you may decide to give in. However, you must bear in mind that your growing puppy will soon take up most of the room, and when he is moulting he will cover every chair with a film of white hairs. You may not mind, but will your visitors appreciate being covered in dog hairs? There is also the possibility that your Dalmatian will claim the best chair as his own, either by refusing to let anybody else sit there, or climbing on behind and trying to push them off – this has happened to me in some Dalmatian homes. If you do not want to battle with your dog, you can compromise by letting your dog have an old chair and putting a washable cover in place.

   Allowing a puppy to sleep on your bed can be a disaster. Apart from the problem of dog hairs, even a giant-sized double bed never seems big enough for a Dalmatian and one human, never mind two. Problems can also occur if the dog becomes jealous of anybody sharing the bed with their 'boss'. If you want your dog to sleep in your bedroom, it is far better that he has his own bed to sleep in.

ANTI-SOCIAL BEHAVIOUR
Young male puppies, even at the age of a few weeks, sometimes get the instinct to

mount their littermates. This is normally associated with the puppies working out their position in the litter, because in the wild, only the most dominant male in the pack would mate the bitches. By the age the puppies leave the litter, this instinct has usually subsided, but occasionally a puppy will continue with this behaviour, even though there are no other puppies around. This behaviour is usually focused on a cushion or blanket, and as soon as you see it happening, you must must stop your puppy with a very firm "No".

If this anti-social behaviour is allowed to continue it will become an increasing embarrassment as the puppy grows older, especially if, instead of a cushion, he chooses your leg or a visitor's leg, or even worse, a young child. Dalmatians are not normally highly-sexed, so this behaviour is the exception – but it must always be dealt with firmly.

BEGGING FOR FOOD
Most Dalmatians love their food, but to preserve your dog's waistline, it is better not to allow him to ask for the food that you are eating, whether at the table or not. Teach your puppy to stay in his bed or another convenient place when it is your mealtime. A puppy can look so appealing, with his large brown eyes gazing at you, as though he hasn't had a square meal for weeks. At times like this it is very hard to ignore the request for just a small crumb from your plate – but if you give in, you have lost the battle forever!

WHO DOES IT BELONG TO?
It is important to teach your puppy to give things up when you ask. Start as soon as your puppy arrives home by making him realise that nothing 'belongs' to him. Occasionally, when your puppy is playing with a toy or eating his food, take it from him. If he objects, tell him "No" in a firm voice, but if he gives the object up without any fuss, be lavish with your praise. Keep the toy or dish for a few seconds and make your puppy sit before you give it back.

Never let children, or anyone else, tease the puppy by taking things from him. This can make a dog become very possessive, and soon he will be reluctant to give up anything without a fight.

JUMPING UP
A Dalmatian will normally greet friends and family in a very boisterous fashion, even if you have only been away for a short time. This is part of the charm of the Dalmatian, but it is better if you can teach your dog not to jump up on these occasions. There may be a day when muddy footprints on your clothes or on your visitors' clothes, are not really appreciated. To stop this bad habit from forming, start off by bending to greet your puppy so that he does not need to lift himself to your height. Then, when you pet him, exert gentle pressure to ensure his feet stay on the ground. Give your dog plenty of fussing, but tell him "No" in firm tones, if he tries to jump up.

REWARDS
For the first few weeks of training, I prefer not to give anything more than plenty of praise as a reward. However, as the puppy gets a little older, he will need more of an incentive to do as you ask, especially when the training becomes more formal. I

When you start formal training, you will find that food rewards are a great help. This Dalmatian is learning to sit, responding to the pressure on his hindquarters, and being rewarded with a tidbit.

When your dog is responding well to the Sit, you can progress to the Down exercise. This Dalmatian is now responding to the command, without the need to pull downwards on his collar.

The Stay routine should be built up gradually. Do not attempt to leave your dog at a distance until you are confident that he understands what is required.

have found that tidbits (Dalmatians love food!) are the answer, but make sure you only use small amounts. It is the thought that counts – your puppy does not need large amounts of food, he just needs to think he is getting something special.

My favourite type of reward to give is liver treats, which are very easy to prepare. My recipe is as follows: cheap liver, sliced and boiled until just cooked through. Cool the liver, then cut it into small pieces or cubes. Spread on a baking sheet and then cook, either under a grill or in the oven, until dry and crisp. I find this keeps well, either in the fridge or freezer, and it handles well in cold and hot weather, without making a mess in your pockets. I only use this as a reward, and the dogs do not have liver at any other time, so to them it is special.

Other treats that can be used are small pieces of chicken, sausages, or cheese – it is a matter of finding something that is right for your dog – and then keeping it as a special reward.

BASIC TRAINING

There are a few basic commands that all dogs should be taught, regardless of whether you want to get involved with formal Obedience training. Your dog must learn to respond to the commands: Come, Sit/Down, Stay, and Heel, in order to be under control and reliable in all situations.

Before you start to train your puppy you must decide what words you are going to use to indicate what you want the puppy to do. It is important to make sure that everybody in the family uses the same words and to try not to change them, as this will only confuse the puppy, especially while he is young.

Try and find a quiet time each day for your training sessions when no other people or animals are around, as your puppy will be easily distracted. The best time is not just after he has woken from a sleep, as he will be too full of energy and bounce at that time. Let him have a short play period and empty himself, and then he will be more receptive when you start training.

"COME"

The attention span of a young puppy is very limited, so formal training can only be for a few minutes each day, but other aspects of elementary training can be incorporated into everyday life in a more relaxed format. Recall training starts with small actions, such as encouraging the puppy to come to you across the room, or to come in from outside, and then rewarding with lots of praise when he does come. To the puppy it will be more of a game, but, in fact, it is basic training.

As the days go by, encourage your puppy to come to you from further away, calling his name and giving the command "Come" when he is out of sight, and always giving lots of praise when he arrives. To start with, it will be a matter of chance whether your puppy comes to you, as he will not really understand what is wanted. However, it will not be long before he makes the connection between the sound of his name and the praise and attention he gets from you. Do not be embarrassed to go down to floor level to praise him, as this is just what a young puppy needs.

"SIT"

Start to use the command "Sit" each time you see your puppy about to sit down of his own accord, as it will start to accustom him to the sound of the word. After a few days, kneel on the floor with the puppy standing in front of you, with his head by your left knee and his tail to the right. Place your left hand in front of your puppy's chest to stop him walking forward, place your right hand on top of his back, just in front of his tail, then gently apply a downward pressure to the right hand, saying "Sit" as the puppy places his bottom on the ground. Repeat this two or three times, remembering to give praise as he does the required sit.

Continue with this exercise until you can feel the puppy sitting without the pressure of your right hand and the restraint of the left hand. Once the puppy has a reasonable idea of what you want him to do, give the command "Sit" as you offer his food. Hold the dish slightly above and in front of his nose, gently press his rump with your right hand, saying "Sit" as before. When he sits, place the dish on the ground before him and then let him eat. Your puppy will soon realise that he needs to sit before he gets his meal.

The next step is to make your puppy Sit on command at other times, not just at his mealtimes, remembering to give plenty of praise whenever he does as you ask. The praise is the most important thing to your puppy, as he instinctively wants to please you.

"STAY"

Once your puppy has learnt to Sit on command, without you gently pushing him into position, then, if you wish, you can extend this part of his training to include Stay. To start the Stay routine, begin when you are giving your puppy his food. Instead of immediately placing his dish on the ground when he sits, wait for a few seconds saying "Staaaay", before placing his food down before him. Slowly increase the length of time you make your puppy wait for the food until he realises that "Stay" is a command.

If your puppy starts to stand up instead of staying in the Sit position, tell him "No" and gently push his rump to the Sit again. At the beginning do not make your puppy wait long for his food as his concentration is not very good. Just wait long enough for your puppy to learn the difference between Sit and Stay.

Once your puppy has learnt this early stage of Stay, you can start to use this command at other times along with the "Sit" command. At first, teach your puppy to Stay as he sits alongside or in front of you, then as he gets older and his Sit and Stay are on command, you can start to teach this as a command to be used at a distance.

To teach this command at a distance, make the puppy sit at your feet facing you, telling him to "Staaaay". Slowly take one step backwards, if your puppy attempts to follow you, tell him "No" and start again. When your puppy stays without coming to you, give him plenty of praise. Increase the training by gradually moving further and further away, but always leave your puppy where he can see you (and you him). Gradually leave your puppy in the Sit, Stay position for longer periods, although at this stage we are still only talking of up to two minutes at a time.

"DOWN"

Teaching the Down is a further step in this series, only to be started when the puppy will easily Sit on command. With the puppy in a sitting position, hold his collar underneath his neck, and with the other hand on his rump to keep it in

Building up concentration is all-important when you are training your dog, and this Dalmatian is behaving impeccably, with all his attention focused on his owner.

Good heelwork is essential in everyday life – not just in competitive obedience.

Agility is an increasingly popular activity, and the athletic Dalmatian finds no difficulty in negotiating the hurdles.

contact with the floor, gently pull the collar down to floor level with the command "Down" (or "Lie"). As with the Sit training, this should only be repeated two or three times in any session, gradually removing the hand from the rump as your puppy becomes more proficient.

As with the Sit, the Down is a natural position for a dog to adopt, so with a little persuasion the puppy will readily accept his "Down" command. Once your puppy needs no assistance from the pull on his collar, add the Down into his Sit, Stay routine. With patience, you should soon be able to train your puppy to stay in either a sitting or lying position, when you move a short distance away.

"HEEL"

Lead-work is a totally different type of training to the other exercises, but it is equally important if you are to enjoy life with a Dalmatian. A fully-grown Dalmatian dog can weigh as much as 75lbs (35kilos), and if that weight is not properly under control when on a lead, you are not going to have an easy time taking your dog for a walk – he will be taking you!

Buying the right collar and lead is the very first step in achieving good Heel-work. To start with, you need a puppy-size collar, and I recommend the soft, woven, nylon type, rather than a leather collar, which tends to be rather stiff and more irritating to a young puppy. To go with the collar, buy a lightweight clip lead.

The first step, once the puppy has settled into the family routine, is to get your puppy used to wearing the collar. Put it on the puppy, not too tightly (you should be able to get at least two fingers between the collar and the puppy's neck) but do not have it too loose or it will slip off over his head. At first the puppy will try to remove his collar, scratching and worrying at it. However, the puppy will soon get used to the feel of the collar and will forget all about it. If your puppy continues scratching at his collar after several days, tell him "No" whenever you see him doing it.

When your puppy has accepted the collar, clip the lead into place and leave him to wander round pulling the lead with him. Tell him "No" if he attempts to chew the lead. Keep an eye on your puppy while he has the lead attached to ensure that he does not get it caught under the furniture. Let your puppy wear the lead in this fashion, for a short time each day, until he obviously accepts it as part of life.

After the lead and collar have ceased to bother your puppy, pick the attached lead off the floor and, holding it in your hand, call the puppy to you, talking to him and encouraging him all the while. At this stage you may find that your puppy objects strongly to wearing the lead, pulling against it, backing away from you, and trying to get the collar over his head. If your puppy does this, gently pull him towards you with the lead, talking quietly to him, giving him reassurance, and when he arrives at your feet, do not forget the praise – even if you have really done all the work.

Continue with this exercise until your puppy comes of his own accord. When he arrives at your feet, start to walk backwards so that the puppy is actually 'walking on the lead', as you give plenty of praise and encouragement. Your puppy may occasionally try to pull away, instead of walking with you. If this happens, stand still, tell him "No", and then encourage him to come to you before continuing with the 'walk'.

Once your puppy is following you when you are facing him, the next step is to turn and walk slowly away from him, so that, in effect, the puppy is following you. Give plenty of encouragement, and if your puppy is at all reluctant, give a quick jerk or pull on the lead (not too hard) and encourage your puppy forward. It can take several days to teach a puppy to walk on the lead, as many do not like the restriction and lack of freedom, but with patience and encouragement on your side, it should not develop into a battle.

The first part of lead training is done at home, both in the house and in the garden, as your puppy will not have completed his vaccination programme. Then, by the time your puppy is ready to go out (usually at three and a half to four months) he will have mastered much of the basic training.

At first, your puppy will pull in all directions, in front, to the side and backward, probably anywhere but where you really want him to go. As the days pass, shorten the lead in your hand – it is customary to walk the dog on your left side – until your puppy is walking by your side, with his head level with your leg. This is the Heel position. When you start to get the puppy into this position, tell him "Heel" in a very firm voice.

If your puppy starts to pull in front of you, either jerk the lead sharply backward saying "Heel" very firmly (in effect, this stops the puppy walking forward, while your next step will bring him at the Heel position again). Alternatively, quickly do an about-turn to the right, which will make the puppy come round behind you and into the Heel position again. Make sure that you give the "Heel" command as he comes into place.

Once you start to take the puppy out for a walk, it is essential that you are in charge, not the dog. Make him walk to heel, and do not let him pull you around. Some owners use a choke-chain (check-chain) when teaching their dog to walk to heel. There is no harm in this, as long as the chain is fitted correctly (with the ring running freely along the top of the chain) which means the chain will release automatically when pressure is released. A dog should never wear a choke-chain constantly; it is a training aid, and should only be used during training sessions or when you are walking your dog.

GOING FOR A WALK
If possible, encourage your puppy to relieve himself in your garden either before you go for a walk or on his return. *Always* make sure that you have some method of disposing of any mess your dog may deposit, (a plastic-bag or a pooper-scooper). Any dog can have an 'accident', but it is your responsibility to clean it up.

As adults, dogs, more than bitches, like to 'mark' their territory, and they will do this by urinating at various places on the walk, usually against a lamppost, tree, wall or anything else that happens to be there, especially if another dog has already left his 'mark'. Allow your dog to sniff and mark a few places on his walk, but do not let him do it to excess.

If you are walking your dog in a residential area, it it a good idea to incorporate some training exercises into the walk, such as teaching him to Sit when you reach a street that you are about to cross, which will prevent him stepping out in front of vehicles. It is also sensible to make your dog Sit if you stop to talk – he is then less likely to greet the other person with possibly muddy feet.

EXERCISING OFF-LEAD
It does not matter how well-behaved your puppy or adult Dalmatian becomes, he should never be exercised off a lead where there is traffic. Even the best dog can

Do not allow your Dalmatian to exercise off-lead until you are confident that he will return to you

behave unpredictably at times, and it only takes a few seconds for an accident to occur. Hopefully, there will parks or fields in your locality where you can safely exercise your dog off-lead. There is nothing more delightful than seeing a Dalmatian running at full speed, but take care not to exercise him in designated children's play areas, restricted sports fields, or any other dog-free areas.

When you first take your young dog to the park, do not let him off his lead immediately. For the first few visits, exercise your dog on his lead so he will learn some of the smells and landmarks, but still be fully under your control. Always walk in the same direction, covering approximately the same ground each time. Take some of your dog's favourite tidbits, and as you go on your walk, give him a piece every now and again, so that he knows they are in your pocket.

After those few visits, it is time to allow your dog to run free. Hopefully, you will have nothing to worry about. Walk part of the way round, giving your dog an occasional tidbit, then undo his lead and let him loose – preferably when there are no other dogs around to distract him. Continue to walk on your usual route, and call your dog to you occasionally, giving plenty of praise and a tidbit when he comes. At about three-quarters of the way through your usual walk, call your dog to you and put him back on the lead, not forgetting the praise and tidbit, then continue home as usual. I have found that teaching a youngster to return in this fashion has brought the best results, as Dalmatians find tidbits very hard to refuse.

THE VERSATILE DALMATIAN

AGILITY
The normal basic training is quite sufficient to make the average family pet into a well-behaved member of the household, ensuring that you will enjoy your Dalmatian. However, because the breed will easily adapt to many ways of life, you may consider other pastimes with your pet, such as competing in Agility or Obedience trials. Of the two, Agility is perhaps the more suitable for the breed. The Dalmatian's natural sense of fun, combined with his speed and quick wits, means that he adapts well to this discipline.

Agility classes are becoming more popular, and it is worth making enquiries to see if there are classes held locally. It is important that all Agility training is supervised by qualified teachers and that all equipment used is safe and of the correct type. You should not start working with your Dalmatian in Agility until he is fully grown – over twelve months of age.

OBEDIENCE
Obedience competitions are far more difficult for a Dalmatian – they do not usually accept the rigid discipline of Obedience work. It is possible to train the breed to the high standards necessary to reach the top Obedience levels, but it needs a great deal of time and patience. It is essential to enrol with a first-class training club, preferably one that has an instructor who understands Dalmatian temperament.

THERAPY DOGS
Because of their natural friendliness towards people, many Dalmatians have become Therapy dogs. These are mature dogs whose behaviour and temperament are of a very high standard, and whose owners volunteer to spend time with their dogs in local hospitals or rest homes. The residents of these homes are not normally allowed pets, but the contact with a dog on a regular basis appears to help with rehabilitation. Local enquiries would establish whether such a scheme is running in your area.

CARRIAGE DOGS
Many people who are interested in horses, also become interested in Dalmatians – there is a definite affinity between the two animals. Because this friendship is easily encouraged, it is not unusual to see Dalmatians running with the horses at pony and trap, or horse and carriage, parades. In competitions, the addition of the Dalmatian to a well-turned-out carriage gives a marvellous air of history to the procession.

Chapter Six

THE SHOW RING

It is important to decide before you buy a puppy whether you are interested in starting to show your dog. Showing, as a hobby, should be good fun and a way of meeting new people who have similar interests as yourself – namely, a love of Dalmatians. However it is also very time-consuming, expensive and frequently addictive. If you get bitten by the show-going bug it can take over your life and before you realise it, you have a house full of Dalmatians and a life full of new friends.

When you first enter the world of dog showing it appears very complicated, but it will become easier to understand as time goes by. All shows are organised by clubs, not by individuals, and each club is affiliated to the national Kennel Club of the country. All shows are run under the rules of that governing body and with its permission.

Each country divides the different breeds into Groups according to the working ability of the breed or its type, e.g. Gundog breeds such as Setters, Spaniels and Retrievers, or Toy breeds such as the Pekingese and Yorkshire Terrier, but the Groups can, and do, vary from country to country in number, names and breeds included. The Dalmatian is a member of the Utility Group in the UK, and a member of the Non-Sporting Group in the USA.

BRITISH SHOWS

There are various types of shows in the UK licensed by the Kennel Club in London. These are: Sanction Shows, Limit Shows, Open Shows and Championship Shows. The Kennel Club is only involved with the choice of judges for Championship shows where Challenge Certificates (CCs) are on offer. In order to become a Champion, a dog must win three CCs under three separate judges. At least one of these CCs must be won after the dog is twelve months old. The Kennel Club is the final court of appeal in any dispute regarding breeding and showing of pure-bred dogs.

AMERICAN SHOWS

The American Kennel Club (AKC) is the governing body in the USA. It is run on similar lines to the Kennel Club in the UK, although there are one or two essential differences. The British club is composed of individual members, whereas the American counterpart is composed entirely of member clubs. It is also responsible for governing dog events in the USA, registration of pure-bred dogs, and maintaining a stud book. There are something like four thousand clubs in America holding licensed shows, but less than fifteen per cent are actually members of the

AKC. In order for a dog to become a Champion, it must win a total of fifteen points, which are determined by the number of dogs competing and by the area of the country where the points are won. In the course of becoming a Champion it is also necessary to annex at least two major wins (three, four or five points) under different judges.

THE SHOW DALMATIAN
Every breed has a written Breed Standard, which is the blueprint of what the breed should be like in appearance and temperament. The Standard varies slightly from country to country but in a breed such as the Dalmatian there are no major differences.

The Dalmatian should be a moderate breed, with no exaggerated points, such as the heavy-coated Poodle or Afghan, or the flat-faced breeds such as the Bulldog and the Pug. However, this does not mean that the Dalmatian does not have 'special' points. It is the markings of a Dalmatian that makes the breed unique. Although many breeds have their own distinctive coat colour, such as the Kerry Blue Terrier, or pattern of markings, such as the Rottweiler or the Yorkshire Terrier, none are as difficult to obtain as the spotting of a Dalmatian.

Almost any Kennel Club registered dog may go into the show ring, but only a few will take top honours, and in Dalmatians there are certain points that are not acceptable in a show dog. It is for this reason that you must tell the breeder, before you buy a puppy, that you are interested in showing, or you could waste a lot of money, time and effort.

UNSUITABLE FOR SHOWING
Some puppies will never be suitable to show because of particular faults, therefore they are normally referred to as 'absolute pets'. These are sometimes sold at a lower price, but it would be false economy to consider buying one, if you are interested in a future show career. These faults are as follows:
1. One or both eyes coloured blue instead of brown.
2. A patch – this is a *solid* area of colour, usually found on the head, around the eyes or ears, but they can be anywhere. It is *not* several spots joined together. A patch can usually be distinguished because there will be *no* white hairs present, and it will feel silky compared with the normal coat.
3. Lemon-spotting – this is not a pale-liver spot but a colour of its onw. It is easy to recognise because the spots are very pale, sometimes almost invisible from across a room, and the nose and eye-rim colour is black.
4. Orange-spotting – not quite as easy to recognise as lemon-spotting, but the spots are definitely orange and not a shade of liver or brown.
5. Spots of more than one colour on the same dog, usually referred to as 'tri-colour'.
6. A large amount of missing pigment – this normally refers to the nose and eye-rim pigment, which should be complete in an adult show dog. Puppies are not usually born with this pigment complete, the colour appears as the puppy grows, but by the time a puppy is of saleable age, i.e. approximately six to eight weeks, it should be at least 75 per cent complete, especially on the blacks. Liver-spotted dogs can be a little slower to show pigment. There may be a small amount of eye-rim missing colour at this age, usually in the corner, but if more than 25 per cent is missing, it is

Show training begins at home. Do not let your training sessions become too long and tedious, or your Dalmatian will never learn to enjoy the show ring.

The show dog must get using to being examined by a stranger, and this includes having his mouth checked to see if he has the correct scissor bite and full dentition.

When you move your Dalmatian in the show ring, the aim is to show an elegant dog with flowing movement.

unlikely that it will ever completely fill with colour. On the nose, small amounts around the edge will probably fill, but large amounts are more doubtful, especially if the flesh at this stage is a very bright pink. If there is a small amount of pigment missing, it will not normally be a great problem in the ring.

Two 'faults' that cannot always be detected at six weeks but will prove a problem for the show ring if found at a later date are:

1. In a male, if either one or both testicles have not descended into the scrotum.
2. If the final adult teeth are not positioned as required in the Standard. The front teeth on a Dalmatian should form what is known as a 'scissor bite', this is where the top teeth are placed immediately over and in front of the lower teeth, when the mouth is closed. Some dogs have their teeth in the reverse position, or with a gap between the upper and lower set. These are not correct.

SHOW POTENTIAL

Nobody can say that a puppy will grow into a show dog, it can only be said that the potential to be a show dog is present at six to eight weeks. For even the best puppy in the litter may go off as he grows. Therefore, having dismissed all the puppies with the above faults because they will never be good enough to show, you will have to choose from the rest of the litter. The best person to advise you on your choice is a responsible breeder, preferably one who has a good record in the show ring. It takes many years and litters to know how a puppy is likely to finish, and even then you cannot always be sure.

Basically, you are looking for a dog that appeals not only to you but to most people. Therefore, the spotting is the next most important feature to look at. Remember that there will probably be more spots to appear over the next few months, and these will be smaller than those already visible. They may show as small shadows under the fur. The later a spot becomes visible, the smaller it usually is. If the spots are very small, they are normally called 'ticks' as opposed to 'spots', and they are not really desirable in a show dog.

Bearing this in mind, a puppy that looks perfectly spotted at six weeks, can finish over-spotted, and if heavily marked at six weeks, it will definitely look even more heavily marked as an adult. However, it pays to also remember that beauty is in the eye of the beholder, and what appeals to one person will not necessarily appeal to all. Try to avoid puppies with large clusters of spots in any one area, or a puppy with too many lines of spots. This type of spotting can appear to alter the shape of the adult dog. When choosing your puppy, go for the colour that you personally prefer. It does not matter in the show ring whether you are showing a black or a liver-spotted dog, as both are fully acceptable, though some judges do show a preference for one or other colour.

An adult Dalmatian should be an elegant dog, capable of good flowing movement with a minimum of effort, but there is no way that this can be seen in a puppy, unless you are a very experienced breeder. You can only make sure that the puppy you buy is in good condition, is well-reared and looks attractive. A hundred and one things can go wrong between buying a puppy and taking him into the ring at six months or later. It can be a case of the swan turning into an ugly duckling – though sometimes it does happen the other way round.

Once you have bought your 'show puppy' remember that whatever happens in the future, he will still be your pet. It will not be the dog's fault, or yours, if he does not make the top spot in the ring – he will still be a loving companion. Showing takes years of patience and dedication – there is rarely instant success.

PREPARING FOR THE SHOW RING

Continue with all the basic training as you would with any puppy, but try to ensure that your puppy meets as many other dogs as possible. Try, if possible, to visit several shows where Dalmatians are classified. This is the best way to see what is expected both of you and the dog in the ring. The best shows to go to are the Dalmatian Breed Club shows or Championship shows, because at these you will see larger numbers of the breed and meet many more people. To start with just watch and learn, ask questions if you are not sure of something, but try not to disturb exhibitors just before they go into the ring.

In many areas there are ring training (ringcraft) classes where exhibitors and newcomers meet to socialise and train their young stock for the ring. (These are not to be confused with Obedience Training classes.) At ring training classes you will learn how to handle your puppy for the ring and even more important, your puppy will learn to be 'handled' by other people, i.e. the judge.

It is most important when you first begin to show a puppy that *he* enjoys his time at the shows, especially when in the ring. To start with, it does not matter if you win or not. While he is a puppy let him play and do his own thing, even in the ring, as long as he is happy – but do not let him interfere with the others in the class. Try to stand your dog still long enough for the judge to see him, even if only for a few seconds. You should not expect a six-month-old Dalmatian to stand like a statue.

It is essential to avoid the trap of training your puppy so intensely that he becomes bored with the whole procedure. A Dalmatian is supposed to be a happy dog, which means tail wagging, eyes twinkling, and ears alert. No dog will look like this if he is bored. There will be time enough when your Dalmatian gets out of the Puppy Class (under twelve months) and into the next class (between one and two years) to let him know that at home he can play, but at the show and in the ring, you expect him to work. The few months of playing will be well worth it. A good, happy Dalmatian will still be giving you 100 per cent in the ring, even when he gets to the Veteran Class.

IN THE RING

All breeders have their own method of showing the breed's best points to the judge, and it is usual for all exhibitors in the breed to use the same method. In the UK and some other countries, Dalmatians are shown free standing. This means on a loose lead, with the dog facing you or standing across the front of you, and the handler rarely touching the dog. In other countries, such as the USA, the Dalmatian is shown stacked. This is where the dog stands across the front of you, but the head and tail are held up in position by the handler.

When showing your dog at any level, the object is to show all his good points and hopefully none of the bad points – there is no such thing as a perfect Dalmatian. Most people are very nervous when they start to show their dog. With many exhibitors, this feeling never really goes away – even the most experienced handler can still have butterflies. Just take a few deep breaths and try to relax, otherwise your tension will travel down the lead and affect your dog.

If you build up a good relationship with your dog, it will be to your advantage when you are competing in the show ring.

The markings on a Dalmatian are of the utmost importance in the show ring, and you must bear this in mind when choosing a puppy with 'show potential.'

LEFT: Good training pays off, and this Dalmatian is showing himself to perfection.

BELOW: Always use a fine slip-lead for showing your dog, and choose a colour which complements your Dalmatian.

Once you get into the ring, you must divide your attention in two directions, firstly to your dog and secondly to the judge. To begin with, you will be directed to stand alongside all the other dogs to be seen in that class. Give yourself and your dog enough space to stand comfortably. Do not crowd others, and do not let other exhibitors crowd you. Make sure that your dog does not interfere with any other dog.

Each dog will be seen in turn by the judge. It is better in the early days if you try to avoid being the first in the line, so you can watch what routine the judge is using and be ready when your turn comes. The judge will 'go over' your dog, with some using their hands more than others. Your job is to ensure that your dog will stand still to allow this, and you must not get in the way of the judge.

Either before or after the individual examination, the judge will ask you to move your dog. The judge is trying to assess your Dalmatian's movement – not yours – so you must make sure that your dog is between you and the judge at all times. You may be asked to move in a straight line away and back, or a triangle, or a circle. Practice all patterns of movement at home. The aim is to move your dog at a medium speed, not too slowly and certainly not at a gallop. Try, if possible, to teach your dog to do this exercise on a loose lead with his head in the air.

After you have been seen by the judge, return to the side of the ring but keep your attention on the judge and make sure that whenever the judge looks in your direction, your dog is looking his best. As the judge is making his final assessment and calling his winners into the centre of the ring, keep one eye on the dog and one on the judge to make sure that you do not miss that call if it comes your way. Do not waste the opportunity by talking to others, talk to your dog.

When you are in the ring, take whatever wins or dismissals come your way with good grace – poor losers and gloating winners are never very popular! Remember that dog showing is only a hobby, and the best dog, your dog, is going home with you whatever happens. Some days you will win when you really should not, and other days you will not be placed when you really should have been. However, there will always be another day and another judge.

DOING THE BEST FOR YOUR DOG

This means presenting your dog in the best way possible. The dog must obviously be in good condition, well-muscled and at the correct weight. This should all be achieved with his normal diet and exercise. After that, the rest is up to you. There are a few simple tips which may come in handy:

1. Always make sure your dog is clean and well-groomed. This does not necessarily mean a bath for each show. With regular grooming, a surface wash with a damp cloth should be enough to keep your Dalmatian clean. Make sure his teeth are clean – the judge will be looking at them – and that his nails are kept short.

2. Use a fine slip-lead for showing your dog – definitely not a heavy chain. Choose a colour that will complement your Dalmatian, and only use that lead in the ring or when training for the ring. In this way your dog will associate the lead with the ring.

3. Wear an outfit that will look clean and smart, and will complement your dog. Plain colours are best, but never wear white trousers or a white skirt or dress in the ring, it will make your dog look dirty. Spotted outfits are good fun but are best left at home, along with high-heeled or noisy shoes.

4. Give yourself adequate time to arrive at the show. If you rush your dog into the

ring, neither of you will give of your best. Ensure that you are ready and waiting when you are due into the ring, since it is very easy to miss your class because you are not concentrating.

5. Remember that your dog does not understand what shows are. He is only trying his best to please you, so do not take your disappointments out on him.

6. Do not show your dog unless he is in good condition and looking well. A miserable, lame dog with a poor coat is going to be penalised by the judge, and remembered by those who may be judging at the next show.

JUDGES

There are two types of judges: breed specialists who normally own and possibly show the breed (or have done so in the past), and non-breed specialists who own or show one or more other breeds. The breed specialist should obviously know the finer points of the breed and usually has a strong view on which aspect of the breed is most important, whereas the non-breed specialist usually takes a broader overall view of the dog. Both types of judges are there to place the dogs in each class in order of preference, according to how closely they conform to the Breed Standard.

When you enter a show, you are really asking for the judge's opinion of your dog when viewed against the others in the class. That opinion can change from day to day, depending on many things. Dogs, like people, can have good days and bad days.

Eventually you may wish to take on the role of a judge yourself. This is not something to be rushed into, so take your time, learn as much as you can about the breed, and remember it is not as easy as it looks from outside the ring. Many of the more experienced non-breed specialists or 'all-rounders' will have judged thousands of dogs, in many breeds, at large numbers of shows, but they will still have started judging in just their own breed at the small shows.

The stud dog you choose must complement your bitch, and you must check that he is free of any inherited conditions.

Chapter Seven

BREEDING DALMATIANS

Dalmatians are without a doubt the most difficult dogs to breed, in respect of producing top-quality puppies that fit the Breed Standard. I was always taught: "If you have one show puppy in a litter, you are lucky. Two show puppies in a litter is a miracle, more than that – you are kennel blind, it is almost impossible!"

Therefore, breeding is one part of owning a Dalmatian that should never be undertaken lightly. Your aim must be to further the interests of the breed, rather than attempt to make money.

RESPONSIBILITIES

MALES
1. Your responsibilities do not end when your dog mates a bitch. You also have to take the responsibility as to whether your dog should mate any particular bitch, or even any bitch at all. No dog should be used at stud unless he is a good, typical Dalmatian, and free from hereditary problems.

If you plan to breed with your bitch she must be fit and healthy, and a typical representative of the breed. You must also take colour inheritance into consideration if you have a liver-spotted Dalmatian.

2. Do not use your dog at stud if he has a patch, a blue eye, if he has only one testicle, or if he is either uni-laterally or bi-laterally deaf.

3. Unless you are intending to provide your male with regular stud work, I would advise against allowing him to mate any bitches. A dog who has never been used at stud will normally not bother about that side of his life. Most dogs destined for a stud career are those whose performance in the show ring confirms they are good, typical, representatives of the breed.

4. Knowing the background to your dog is important. No dog has a perfect pedigree, there are always problems hidden somewhere. Therefore, care must be taken not to mate a bitch who has a background with similar hidden problems.

5. However good your dog looks, *never* use him at stud if he is at all aggressive or nervous, and *never* let him mate a bitch with a poor temperament.

FEMALES

Breeding a litter from your bitch is hard work, time-consuming, and initially expensive – there is a lot of expense before you get to sell your puppies. Therefore, there are many things to consider before you decide to breed from your bitch, the most important being:

1. Why do I want to breed a litter?
2. Do I have the facilities to whelp and rear a litter?
3. Can I cull puppies from the litter if it is necessary?

If you are considering breeding a litter purely to raise money, I would seriously advise you not to do so. It is very easy for things not to go as you plan, and you could finish with some very large bills from the vet and no puppies to sell. Breeding can be, and usually is, a very risky endeavour.

Assuming that you really do want to have a litter from your bitch, you must also consider whether or not she is good enough to breed from. It is not necessary for a bitch to be a top class show winner to be good enough to have a litter, but there are certain 'faults' that should never be present in a brood bitch. Never breed from a bitch with the following faults:

1. An aggressive or nervous temperament.
2. Total (bi-lateral) or partial (uni-lateral) deafness.
3. A patch of solid colour.
4. Any hereditary problem.
5. Any other colour but black or liver-spotted.
6. It is also preferable that you do not breed from a blue-eyed bitch.

One final consideration is the necessity of culling puppies. There are occasions when puppies *must* be culled – sometimes within the first hours, or sometimes at around five or six weeks. Nobody enjoys having to do this, but with a Dalmatian litter it can be a necessity. If you feel that you cannot take on this responsibility (aided by your vet), then you must not embark on breeding a litter of Dalmatian puppies.

THE IN-SEASON BITCH

Assuming that you still want to breed from your bitch, you must look upon it as a long-term venture and start, even while she is still a puppy herself, to consider all it entails.

Dalmatian bitches vary tremendously as to the frequency of their seasons. Some may have their first season at six months and continue with a six-monthly cycle, while others may be fifteen months before their first season, following on with a very irregular cycle. The average age for the first cycle is around eight months, usually followed by an eight or nine-month cycle.

As your puppy reaches the six to seven month age, watch for any changes in the vulva (this is the opening through which your bitch urinates). As she comes into season, the vulva becomes swollen and she will begin to show a pink fluid discharge. A season lasts for approximately twenty-one days. The discharge will become heavier and a brighter red over the first week to ten days.

Most bitches are ready for mating during the middle part of the season (on average, between the tenth and twelfth days). It is essential that the bitch is not allowed to run with any male dog at this time – except when a mating has been arranged. In the latter part of the season the bitch's vulva will start to return to its normal size, and the discharge will lessen and then cease.

Before you consider mating your bitch, you must ensure that she is fully fit, not carrying excess weight, and free from all infections, (including any internal vaginal infections). A routine check from the vet is the best plan. Dalmatians should not really be mated until they are at least eighteen months old, as before that age they are still too immature to do justice to a litter.

CHOOSING A STUD DOG

If you bought your puppy from a reputable breeder, ask his or her advice as to which dog or dogs would be most suitable for your bitch, and ask reasons as to why those dogs would be best. You will need to find a dog that complements your bitch, both on paper (his pedigree) and in terms of his general appearance. Try to find a dog to improve on any faults your bitch may have – never use a dog that has the same faults, because that would then accentuate those same faults in the puppies.

COLOUR INHERITANCE

You do not *have* to use a dog of the same spotting colour as your bitch, but bearing colour in mind, decide which you would prefer. I will not attempt to explain the complexities of colour inheritance in Dalmatians. But the following is a useful guideline. Black spots can be produced by either a dominant black (BB) or a hybrid black (Bb) gene. The liver spots are produced by the pure recessive (bb) gene. Therefore:

1. Two livers mated together will produce all liver puppies.
2. A black to a liver will sometimes produce some liver puppies in the litter.
3. A black to a black will usually produce black puppies, but sometimes can produce a liver puppy.

A dominant black (BB), which can only be proven over a long period of test matings and their resultant puppies, can only produce black-spotted puppies, irrespective of whether mated to a black or liver. A 'recessive' black (Bb), however, can produce liver puppies if mated to a liver or another recessive black.

Once you have decided upon the dog you prefer, and assuming his owner is willing to accept your bitch for service, discuss and agree on the terms of the mating with the stud dog owner. Most proven stud dogs (dogs that have previously sired litters) have their stud fee paid at the time of the mating. If the dog is a maiden (unproven), the fee is sometimes not paid until the puppies arrive.

Dalmatian puppies are born white. This litter is just two days old.

By ten days old, the spots are beginning to appear, and the eyes are starting to open.

ABOVE: Dalmatians make good mothers, and will care for all the puppies' needs for the first two weeks of their lives.

RIGHT: By four weeks the puppies are emerging as individual personalities.

THE MATING

As soon as you notice that your bitch's season has started, contact the stud dog owner to confirm arrangements. The normal procedure is for the bitch to travel to the dog, and you will need to judge the best time for mating. Most vets will test in-season bitches, if requested, to determine when they will be ready to mate. I have recommended this test for many years, especially if the dog and bitch lived a long way from each other, and on almost every occasion the mating has been quick, easy, and resulted in puppies.

Even if you do not wish to make use of this testing, I would recommend a visit to the vet at the start of the season, to ensure that your bitch is not carrying any vaginal infections that could be transferred to the stud dog. When the day comes to take your bitch to be mated, keep her as calm as possible and make sure before you leave home that she has relieved herself outside.

If your journey is a long one, ensure that she has time to urinate before she is introduced to the dog. Every stud dog owner has his or her own way of working their dog. Some will have an area outside where the mating will take place, others will stay inside, some require your help with the bitch, others do not – all will have their own routine.

When the bitch is initially introduced to the dog, she may well appear aggressive towards him, but do not panic at this stage, it is perfectly normal. Provided your bitch is presented for mating on the correct day, this initial apparent aggression will soon disappear. She will start to allow the dog to court her, until she is ready to 'stand' with her tail fully round to the side, ready for the dog to mount and mate her.

Once this mating is finished, the dog and bitch will still remain tied together for some time. At this point, the dog will normally dismount and turn to stand tail to tail with the bitch. Some dogs will only dismount with their front legs and, in effect, stand side by side with the bitch. The tie can last for just a few minutes, or for much longer (ties of over an hour can happen, but ten to twenty minutes is more usual). It is during this time that you could be asked to hold your bitch steady, to discourage her from trying to pull away and possibly injuring the dog.

THE IN-WHELP BITCH

Once the mating has taken place, make sure that your bitch is kept away from all other male dogs until her season is finished – probably for another ten to twelve days. The gestation or pregnancy normally lasts for nine weeks (sixty-three days), and puppies usually arrive within a few days, either side of that time.

For the first few weeks after the mating, the bitch needs no extra rations or delicate handling, life should go on as normal. If you wish to confirm whether or not she is in whelp, most vets can give an indication at four and a half to five weeks after mating, though this is by no means 100 per cent accurate. It is also possible in some areas to arrange for electronic pregnancy scanning at around six weeks, when any whelps present would be visible on the screen.

Assuming that your bitch is carrying pups, a slight increase in feed can be given from about five weeks. This should entail feeding a higher percentage of protein, rather than carbohydrate. You must make sure that your bitch does not put on excess fat especially around her stomach and ribs – if she does it will hinder her at whelping time.

As your bitch becomes larger and more rotund, reduce any strenuous exercise and ensure that she is not allowed to jump over or on to anything high. By about seven weeks, she should be becoming quite heavy, especially if she has a large number of pups to carry. She will need slightly more good-quality food, but not excessive quantities. If she is getting very large, it will be better to give her several small meals each day, rather than one or two large meals which will make her feel uncomfortable.

You should decide where your bitch is to have her pups before you undertake to mate her, though she will not need to occupy that space until about a week before the pups are due. The whelping area needs to be a minimum of three feet by four feet (one metre square approx), dry, draught-free, with a room temperature of 75 degrees Fahrenheit. You will also need space for the puppies once they reach four/five weeks of age.

THE WHELPING

EARLY LABOUR
About a week to ten days prior to the due date of whelping, move the bitch from her usual sleeping area into her whelping area. As she gets close to whelping her body temperature will start to fall and she will probably start to rip the paper bedding to shreds and make a nest in the box. She will become very restless, standing up, turning round, then re-making her nest before lying down again, and she may start to pant a little. The bitch may spend considerable time licking the area around her vulva, which will have enlarged and become very soft. She may in the last few hours refuse food. All these signs are the first part of her labour.

THE DELIVERY
The next stage of labour is when the bitch starts to push or bear down in earnest. She will probably lie panting in between the contractions, and as one begins she will brace her back and hindquarters. As a puppy is about to be born, the sac in which it is enclosed will start to appear from the bitch's vulva, but will withdraw back inside once or twice before the main contraction will expel it from the bitch. There will probably be a rush of watery fluid from the bitch, along with the puppy and its sac, and the afterbirth will follow.

Normally the bitch will immediately start to clean the puppy, tearing the sac and removing all the debris and fluids she has expelled, including the afterbirth, from the puppy. If the bitch does not make any attempt to clean the puppy – sometimes first-time mothers are frightened or just do not know what to do – encourage her to lick the puppy. If she still refuses, briskly rub the puppy dry with a towel. Do not worry if Mum appears to be rather rough with her puppy, it is necessary to get the puppy breathing and empty the fluids from the airways.

Subsequent puppies may arrive at regular intervals of maybe twenty minutes or longer, each preceded by a session of contractions or pushing, or there may be longer intervals of up to an hour and a half between pups arriving. The bitch will appear to have a short rest from contractions between each birth. However, if the bitch appears to be having full contractions and is pushing hard, for maybe an hour, without a puppy being born, then call the vet. There may be a puppy in a wrong position or some other problem which requires professional help. Do not attempt to interfere with the bitch yourself, you could do more harm than good.

This litter of six is now completely weaned. At six weeks their markings are now clearly visible, and you can get some idea of how they will look as adults.

The puppies will increasingly start to play with each other and explore their surroundings. This is another important stage in the rearing process.

POST WHELPING

Once all the pups appear to have arrived, the bitch will settle down for a short but well-earned rest, having washed and cleaned all her family. At this stage offer her some warm milk with a little glucose or honey added. (If the labour is lengthy, offer a drink while she is resting between pups.)

You can now take your bitch outside to empty herself, although some mothers are very reluctant to go, and so you must be quite firm. While she is out of the box, remove all the old papers and replace them with dry bedding. For the first few days the bitch will be very reluctant to leave her pups for any reason, even to eat or drink. You must be very firm with her and take her out at regular intervals to relieve herself, taking the chance to clean the box each time. The bitch will continue to have a discharge – bright-red at the start but gradually becoming darker – for about three weeks.

I have described a textbook scenario of whelping, and hopefully your bitch will not experience any problems. However, it is advisable to read as much as you can on the subject so you are aware of difficulties that can arise. Better still, ask an experienced breeder to be with you during the whelping, and then you will have expert help on hand if it is needed.

CARING FOR THE BITCH AND PUPPIES

FEEDING

After the bitch has had her rest, you will probably need to give her a light feed, such as scrambled eggs or rice pudding, as new mothers will not always take their normal food at this point. If you can, provide her with a diet specially formulated for lactating bitches (bitches feeding a litter). It will have all the necessary minerals etc. for her to maintain good health while producing large quantities of milk. If such food is not available, ensure that your bitch has a well-balanced, good-quality, high protein diet. She must also be provided with large amounts of fluids to drink, to maintain milk production.

The amount of extra food and fluids that the bitch will need, gradually increases from the birth up to about the third or fourth week after the birth. She could require up to about three times her normal amount, especially if feeding a large litter. As the puppies start to be weaned away from their mother, her food and fluid intake should be gradually reduced, and by the time the puppies are fully weaned at about six weeks, she should be back to her normal diet.

For the first two weeks all you really need to do is keep the whelping box and occupants clean. The bitch will normally do all the rest, feeding and cleaning her pups. At about three and a half weeks, start to introduce the puppies to other food. This is the start of weaning them off their mother. I have always started this with a small amount of meat – good-quality chopped beef, cooked and pureed in an electric food blender, and then cooled.

Take each puppy in turn, and on a well-covered knee/lap introduce the puppy to a small dish of the meat by touching the mixture to the puppy's muzzle. Most puppies will start to lap this mixture quite readily, but some need a little persuasion, and either way they will only take a very small amount. Repeat this procedure several times during the day until the puppies lap at the meat with ease. Commercial feeds specifically for weaning puppies can be used at this stage, following the manufacturer's instructions. Once the puppies are readily lapping at food, usually within two or three days, give larger amounts of the meat puree, twice a day, morning and evening. At this point start to introduce a milk and cereal meal, once, then twice, a day, lunchtime and bedtime. The meals at this point can either be fed individually to each puppy, or in one or two communal shallow dishes.

Discuss with your vet a worming regimen for both your bitch and her puppies, starting before you mate her. The change in hormone levels in a pregnant bitch appears to activate the dormant eggs carried in most bitches, resulting in both mother and puppies having a worm burden. All puppies should be treated for worms before being sold.

ASSESSING YOUR LITTER

When the puppies are first born, before their mother cleans and dries them, it is possible to see the spotting on the skin. This gives an indication of the pattern of spots that the dog will have when an adult (sometimes, not all those skin spots will emerge as full spots through the coat). Once the bitch cleans the puppy, these spots disappear leaving the puppy with a white coat.

If, after the bitch has dried the pup, there is a area of solid colour on the coat, this is what is referred to as a patch, highly undesirable in a Dalmatian. Because it is so undesirable, and is an hereditary fault, many Dalmatian breeders arrange with their vet to cull any patched puppies, especially if they have a large litter. If you do not cull these puppies, they should be sold without papers and most definitely not for breeding purposes.

The true spots begin to appear through the coat from about eight to ten days, a few hairs at a time. Each day will bring a change to the puppies and they will soon become easily-recognised individuals. Skin pigment on the nose and eye-rims can sometimes be present at birth. If not, it will start to appear as the days go by, just one or two small dots at first, then gradually filling over all the area.

When the puppies' eyes first open, they will all appear to be blue. If this is a dark-blue, it will slowly change to brown, (usually, the darker the blue, the darker the brown will be). However, if the eye is a bright sky-blue, then it will always be a blue-coloured eye. Sometimes an eye can be part-blue, part-brown. This is normally referred to as a blue-fleck.

DETECTING DEAFNESS

Deafness is a major problem in the breed, and any responsible breeder should test every litter to see if any of the puppies are affected. There are three levels of hearing in the breed:
NORMAL HEARING: A dog that can hear in both ears.
UNI-LATERAL DEAFNESS: A dog that is deaf in one ear.
BI-LATERAL (TOTAL) DEAFNESS: A dog that is deaf in both ears.

The only way to be certain of the level of hearing in a dog is to machine-test as you cannot detect uni-lateral deafness by any other means at present. Many breed clubs have official testing schemes in operation, and all responsible breeders have their stock tested.

All bi-laterally/totally deaf puppies should be culled. They should not be kept, sold or given away. They can never enjoy the normal life of a hearing Dalmatian, and if such a dog ever escaped or got lost, he would stand a grave risk of being involved in an accident because he would not be able to hear traffic. Do not shirk your responsibility: consider the future welfare of that dog.

Uni-laterally deaf puppies are perfectly acceptable as pets, but they should never be bred from. Research has shown that breeding from normal-hearing parents lessens the incidence of deafness in the offspring, but breeding from uni-laterally or bi-laterally deaf parents increases the incidence of deafness in the offspring. Genetic research is continuing into deafness in dogs and it is hoped that one day 'carriers' of the problem will be identifiable and eliminated from future breeding programmes.

SELLING YOUR PUPPIES

When potential purchasers enquire about your puppies, remember all the questions that you were asked before you bought your own puppy, and do not be afraid to ask those same questions. The future safety, happiness and well-being of your litter is in your hands.

Dalmatians are a hardy, no-nonsense breed, and with a good diet and regular exercise, your dog should have few health problems.

Chapter Eight

HEALTH CARE

The Dalmatian is a robust, hardy dog, with few health problems. With a well-balanced diet and regular exercise, your dog should live a long life with few visits to the vet, other than routine trips for booster inoculations. However, all responsible owners should be aware of the more common canine ailments and canine parasites in order to keep their dogs in peak condition.

GENERAL CARE

BLOAT/TORSION
Bloat occurs occasionally in medium-sized dogs, shortly after feeding. The stomach fills rapidly with gas, swelling and sometimes also twisting (gastric torsion). The dog is in great pain, breathing is difficult, and he may retch but not vomit. This is an emergency situation and veterinary help must be sought immediately, as even a few seconds delay can have a fatal result. There is no definite cause of this condition, but drinking excess water after dry food, rough exercise soon after a meal, too large a meal, or even a large intake of air with the meal (such as with a greedy, rapid eater) could all be contributory factors. It is therefore a good idea to check your dog once or twice after meals, if he is not normally with you.

FLEAS
Fleas are usually obvious on a Dalmatian coat, but even if you cannot see any, you should give a regular anti-flea treatment on a routine basis. This is particularly important during the summer months, and is easy to do using suitable sprays or shampoos. Fleas also live in carpets, bedding etc. (especially if you have a centrally-heated home), so it is also necessary to wash the dog's bedding and treat all the places where your dog usually lies. Fleas are hosts to the larvae of other parasites so they must be eliminated.

INOCULATIONS
The initial puppy inoculations give cover against disease for approximately one year. A future 'booster' regimen should be discussed with your vet, as some diseases are more prevalent in some areas and therefore need greater cover. Most boosters are given annually.

SICKNESS AND DIARRHOEA
If your dog starts to pass very loose stools or vomits (other than if he has eaten a

little grass and brought that back along with a little bile), do not feed him for twenty-four hours, just leave him cooled, boiled water to drink – definitely no milk – then give him a small light meal. In many cases, this action will stop the problem.

WORMING

Your puppy should have been thoroughly wormed before you bought him, but a change in environment can produce a small problem again. It is best to worm your puppy two weeks after you get him, and again ten days later. Thereafter, a worming routine every six months should keep your dog relatively free of worms. Preparations for worming come in many forms, liquid, tablets, or granules. Ask your vet for advice.

Always follow the instructions, and ensure that you are using the correct preparation for the problem. There are three common types of worms:

ROUNDWORMS: These are the most common, and most puppies carry a roundworm burden. They look similar to a piece of white spaghetti, two or three inches long, and are usually found in the stools.

TAPEWORMS: These look similar to large grains of rice, and are usually found on the hair around the anus.

HOOKWORMS: This type of worm is common is some countries, and your vet will advise on the correct treatment.

There is a slight chance of infection by worm larvae to humans, especially to children, therefore it is important that dogs are kept free of all internal parasites, and children should be taught basic hygiene when around dogs.

TIMES TO CONSULT THE VET

1. If there is any rapid loss of weight.
2. If there is vomiting or diarrhoea that continues after the treatment described above, especially if any blood is present in the stools.
3. If the dog refuses food for more than a day (Dalmatians rarely refuse food without reason).
4. If there is bleeding from the penis or discharge from the vulva (other than the bitch's season).
5. If there is any lameness that does not clear within a few days.
6. If there is excessive drinking, except that caused by very hot weather.
7. If there is any bleeding from the mouth or gums, especially if the breath is smelling very strongly.
8. If there is any marked change in behaviour.

If you ever have that gut feeling that there is a problem, always remember that your dog has not read the medical books, and his symptoms and reactions may not be as listed in the textbook. Your feeling or instinct may save your dog a lot of distress, if you act upon it rather than dismiss it!

INHERITED PROBLEMS

CANCER

Unfortunately, cancer appears to be diagnosed more frequently in the breed, and the tendency does appear to run in families. Treatments such as chemotherapy and radiotherapy are becoming more commonly available, but sometimes euthanasia is the only answer.

DEAFNESS

Dalmatians are acknowledged to have the highest percentage of hearing problems, in any breed of dog. There are thirty-seven breeds known to have a hearing problem, and research has shown that approximately twenty-five per cent of Dalmatian puppies born are affected. (See Chapter 7: Breeding Dalmatians.)

ENTROPION

Unlike some other breeds, Dalmatians are not listed as having any hereditary eye problems, although entropion, which is one or both eyelids turning inwards, can occur. The irritation caused by the eyelashes on the eye can cause ulceration of the cornea and be very painful. If you notice your Dalmatian developing runny eyes, ask your vet for advice. If the condition is severe, it requires surgery. This is a simple operation, and is entirely successful as far as the dog is concerned. However, a dog who has entropion or any other eye problems, should not be bred from.

HIP DYSPLASIA

This is a malformation of the ball-and-socket joint which forms the hip joint. It can lead to varying degrees of lameness and discomfort, depending upon the extent of the malformation. The condition is hereditary, but environmental circumstances can also affect the dog. It is therefore advisable to ensure that your puppy does not carry too much weight, does not play excessively on slippery surfaces, and does not run up and down stairs while he is growing. Young bones and joints are easily damaged.

It is possible to X-ray to check for this condition, and official schemes are in operation. These X-rays are scored, and any dog with a high score should not be used for breeding.

KIDNEY AND URINARY TRACT PROBLEMS

Some Dalmatians can have problems in this area, in as much as they can form 'kidney stones' due to an inability to absorb protein correctly from their diet. Provided the problem does not become too severe, it can normally be kept under control by a special diet and sufficient fluid intake. If your dog appears to be having difficulty passing urine or the urine is blood-stained, take your dog to the vet, preferably taking a specimen of his urine with you. Males are more likely to be affected than females. This problem appears to run in families and is not widespread throughout the breed.

SKIN PROBLEMS

Many Dalmatians do suffer from skin problems, often referred to as 'Dally rash'. The most common appearance of this is inflammation of the skin, followed by the formation of pustules (oedema), which will usually come to a 'white head' but can sometimes just stay as lumps under the skin. This is usually followed by the hair in the area becoming stained – white hairs becoming a pink to dirty-brown colour with a waxy type coating – or a noticeable loss of hair in the area. Sometimes a Dalmatian will have discoloured hair followed by baldness. It will take at least one complete moult to eradicate this discoloured hair.

As your dog gets older, make sure he enjoys his remaining years in comfort.

The underlying cause is usually the demodex mite, which lives in the hair follicle. Normally these are present in small numbers and cause no problem to the dog's natural immune system. However, if these numbers suddenly increase, an outbreak of Dally rash occurs because the immune system can no longer deal with the situation. This sudden increase or imbalance can be brought about by many causes, including stress, and sometimes even a small scratch or cut in the area. Spring and early summer are the most common times for outbreaks to occur.

The mite is originally passed from mother to pup, mainly during the first few days after birth. Young dogs may grow out of the problem with maturity, as their immune systems fully mature, but if demodex suddenly appears in the adult dog, unless it is quickly treated, it can be difficult to overcome. The top of the head is frequently the first area for Dally rash to appear, but it can occur anywhere on the dog.

If the reason for the sudden imbalance can be found and eliminated, there may be the possibility of preventing further problems. Most of the treatments available only deal with the resulting Dally rash and its clearance. The mites can, on occasion, be very difficult to locate, sometimes needing deep skin scrapes or biopsies to obtain a result. Because the dog's immune system is depressed during these outbreaks, steroids should not be used in the treatment of Dally rash.

There is little risk of the mite transferring between adult dogs (or to humans), but because of the passage between mother and pup, you should not breed from a bitch with the problem, unless it has been eradicated.

CONCLUSION
It is difficult to describe life with a Dalmatian in the pages of a book. There may be times when it seems hard work, especially when you are learning to cope with a headstrong youngster, but with a little time, patience, and lots of love, you will be rewarded with a loyal and true companion for many years to come. The Dalmatian is a lovely breed, elegant in looks and happy in life – a great addition to every family.